HENRY WINKLER TALKS ABOUT:

MARRIAGE
"If I'm going to bring life into this world with the help of a woman, and if I'm going to have any kind of rapport with that woman or with that child, I'd better be exactly who I am. . . . It is my hope that when I do marry it'll be a one-time experience."

SUCCESS
"I haven't done it all by myself. I couldn't have done it without Ron Howard. There's no way I could have done it without him. I couldn't have done it without Tom Miller or Garry Marshall."

HIS FIRST REAL LOVE
"She had dark hair with a blonde streak in the front and I fell in love! I want to tell you! I lived down the block from her, and I saw her about 24 hours a day. I wrote her 150 letters trying to put into words exactly what it was that I felt for her."

HIS SCHOOL GRADES
"For a long time I thought I was stupid, which was very painful."

DANCING
"I think dancing is the second greatest physical action a human being can engage in."

THE FONZ: The Henry Winkler Story is an original POCKET BOOK edition.

THE FONZ

The Henry Winkler Story

by CHARLES E. PIKE

PUBLISHED BY POCKET BOOKS NEW YORK

THE FONZ: THE HENRY WINKLER STORY

POCKET BOOK edition published September, 1976

2nd printing....................August, 1976

This original POCKET BOOK edition is printed from brand-new
plates made from newly set, clear, easy-to-read type.
POCKET BOOK editions are published by
POCKET BOOKS,
a division of Simon & Schuster, Inc.,
A GULF+WESTERN COMPANY
630 Fifth Avenue,
New York, N.Y. 10020.
Trademarks registered in the United States
and other countries.

ISBN: 0-671-80746-3.

Interior design by Cathy Vallila

Printed in the U.S.A.

For Henry,
   because he is who he is,
And to Mickey,
   because she made it possible.

CONTENTS

16 pages of photos appear between pages 64
and 65.

INTRODUCTION

Long after The Fonz made him rich and famous, a superstar who traveled with three bodyguards, Henry Winkler continued to live in his small and usually cluttered West Los Angeles apartment. It was a one-bedroom unit, with a small bath and a living room-dining room combination. A furnished apartment, it was outfitted with Henry's double bed, a beanbag chair, a television, and portable stereo.

From the one front window you could see the heated pool in the courtyard. The window decorated the dining area, which also held a glass-topped table and four matching chairs. The potted plants covering the table made it obvious that Henry seldom ate at home. Most of the plants were still in their original plastic containers, the price tags stuck to their sides.

Henry moved back and forth from a green canvas director's chair to the kitchen, brewing himself a cup of tea as we talked. He was barefoot, wearing cut-off jeans and a T-shirt. Unshaven, his hair falling to one side, he looked very much like he'd gotten out of bed just before I'd arrived. But he was his usual wide-awake, articulate self discussing the tough-talking, motorcycle-riding high-school dropout he plays on TV.

"The Fonz," Henry Winkler said with a hint of his native New York creeping into his voice. "Well, one of the things he shows is that you can be cool from your center. You can be cool from integrity. You don't have to carry a chain around to beat anybody's brains in. That's a sign of weakness. Any kind of physical force is a sign of weakness, unless you are defending your life.

"So The Fonz is cool based on strength of character rather than strength of muscle. He has his own morality. He is a fair human being because he wants to be dealt with fairly. But don't mess with him—do not.

"The Fonz likes to be admired, but he can back up that admiration. You see, he never claims to do anything he can't do. He's not full of hot air because the bigger you are the harder you fall. The man who tells you who he is, is never who he tells you he is. The Fonz can say he's cool because he *is* cool."

The Fonz. His full name is Arthur Fonzarelli, but his friends call him Fonzie. Henry Winkler has been playing him to perfection on the ABC-TV series, *Happy Days*. Henry's portrayal of the leather-jacketed 1950s culture hero has turned the show around from 48th place to the top ten. In the process, Henry himself has received an Emmy nomination, 3000 fan letters a week, an invitation from the Hell's Angels to join the club, and national cultdom.

Tanya Tucker, the sexy young singer, sports a "Happy Days" T shirt and kids *Crawdaddy* Magazine, "I want a date with da Fonz." *People* Magazine reports, "The Fonz is a smash . . . he's TV's super-character . . . Henry Winkler has cast a giant shadow on the land." Aaaaay!

The man behind The Fonz is conspicuously different from the characterization that's made him so famous. "Fonzie's not me," Henry has said. "The Fonz is my fantasy, and I want people to know there *is* a Henry Winkler—and who he is."

Rock star Phoebe Snow provides an interesting insight into the real Henry Winkler. Once on "The Dinah Shore Show," Henry had mentioned that Phoebe was the woman he respected more than any other—besides Dinah herself. Phoebe says, "I heard about what he'd said and thought, 'That's really nice. Even though I don't know him, I'm going to call him.' So I did, and I left a message with his answering service. And I thought, 'Well, that's it. That's Hollywood, with an answering service and everything.'

"Twenty minutes later I get this phone call back and this man's voice says, 'Who is this, really?' And I told him, and he said, 'Really?'

Like he was afraid I was somebody else. Then we got into this nice conversation, and because we're both from the same basic area of New York I felt this kinship with him. In no time at all I felt like I'd been talking to him for years— very relaxed, very comfortable.

"So we're basically phone buddies. I've never met him, but I'm moving out there, so I hope we'll get to meet soon."

That first phone call has since been followed by other lengthy telephone conversations, including some about a brief illness the singer's baby, Valerie, suffered shortly after her birth.

"We've had some personal problems and I'm afraid I dumped it all on him," Phoebe says. "Sometimes I called him when I was really depressed, and he just took it all in stride. He'd say, 'That's all right. Get it out; tell me about it.'

"I really dig him as a person. It's hard to pinpoint why we had this sudden rapport, because it's like he's the faceless voice and the voiceless face. But we rap about life in general as if we'd been doing it all our lives; we say whatever's on our minds.

"In my new album I'm going to do a little musical tribute to Henry. It's just a small one, but it's my way of expressing to him that I really appreciate his friendship."

David Ackroyd, appearing on daytime TV's "Another World," is an old friend who'd worked with Henry in the Yale Repertory Company.

Henry, David, and David's wife Ruth shared a house in East Hampton one summer with eleven other aspiring young actors. David remembers Henry's efforts on behalf of the Ackroyds' lost cat, made all the more memorable by Henry's active dislike of felines.

"Even though he couldn't stand that animal," David says, "because the cat belonged to us, he really went out of his way to take care of it and see that we got it back. That typifies Henry— he's a very loyal friend."

Then there's Henry Winkler as Henry sees him. Which begins our story . . .

—CHARLES E. PIKE

CHAPTER 1

"I Am Not a Little Rich Kid Making Gooa"

"My father was born in 1903 in Budapest," Henry says. "He started working for Ernst Zeidleman Corporation, a lumber company, as a messenger when he was about fifteen or sixteen years old. When he was thirty, Ernst handed him the company, made him take it over.

"It's a spectacular thing my father did. He picked up the company and he moved it to Holland when they were forced to flee Berlin. And then he picked it up and moved it to the United States. That's an unbelievable feat in itself!

"But I am not a little rich kid making good. My father worked very hard. Within months after he and my mother arrived in this country, he earned enough money to buy back the family jewelry he had had to hock, but that doesn't mean he was rich.

"I don't know where that ever got started, that I come from a wealthy family. My father believes in a Spartan mind and a Spartan body. He also believes that education is incomplete without traveling, so what he did with the money he made was take his family on a lot of trips."

To afford these trips, the Winkler home was a modest apartment in midtown Manhattan; Henry's parents still live there today. Thirty years ago the area was considered a middle-class, "nice" neighborhood.

"It's not so fancy now," Henry says. "Our place is a comfortable one-level apartment on the tenth floor; I lived there until I got to graduate school. My father also bought a vacation home

in upstate New York where we went on week-
ends during the summer. But my father had to
hustle in order to maintain the life he built for
his family. He had to work very hard so his
family could have a good life.

"There were a lot of kids with European
parents in our neighborhood," Henry remembers. "Traditionally that meant there was always
someone with us while our parents were being
productive. I had a nanny because my father was
at work and my mother was involved in com-
munity functions, or they would be traveling
together. My father traveled a lot because of his
business, but I was certainly brought up by my
parents."

His parents enrolled their son in public school,
primarily for the purpose of meeting kids from
different cultural backgrounds.

"I went to a public school right up the street
from our home, P.S. 87," Henry says. "It was a
predominantly Jewish neighborhood, but the
school had kids from a number of other areas.
We had blacks, Puerto Ricans, everybody. In the
seventh grade, I was sent to private school. But
that was only because its educational system was
better. As I said, my father is crazy about education."

His father's insistence that Henry do well in
school was probably the very reason he didn't
get particularly good marks. School was seldom

Henry's favorite spot—with occasional exceptions.

"Mrs. Balingson," Henry sighs, "was beautiful. She was my fourth grade teacher, and the aunt of one of my very first girl friends, Lynn. Lynn lived in the country, near the summer home my family had. I was friendly with her brother, Andy, and I remember I gave her an expandable identification bracelet. That was the first event of its kind.

"And the first kiss I ever had," Henry says with a grin, "was from a little girl who went to P.S. 87, with me. I kissed her when we were in the fourth grade, and we were standing under a flight of stairs in the apartment building where I lived.

"When I kissed her I knew this was going to be around for a long time. I discovered that kissing is good.

"My best friend. He lived on the fourth floor and I lived on the tenth and top floor of the same building. And from the first through the sixth grades we had a string from my apartment to his apartment, diagonally across the outside of the building, and I would send down a milk container that would go inside his bedroom window, hit his train, and knock the cars into a box. That way he knew I was trying to reach him, and he'd come to the window and we would decide what to do for the day."

Unfortunately, the system only worked one

way—Henry's. If Leland wanted to contact Henry he'd have to climb six floors to the Winkler apartment. Nevertheless the friendship flourished.

"One day, I had gotten this chemistry set," Henry says, "and we did this whole thing in a test tube. It started to smoke so we threw it over the side of the building into the courtyard below. Well, just as we did that my mother called us for lunch, so we had to obediently sit down to eat. But right afterward we went downstairs to find it and discovered we'd made some kind of rubber substance. We could never reproduce it though because we didn't know what the hell it was. But it sure was rubbery."

CHAPTER 2

"You Were Born
to Be an Actor"

When Henry was eight, he saw Alfred Hitchcock's suspense-shocker *Rear Window* and, to hear him tell it, it affected the rest of his life.

"I'd look up at the screen and think, 'How am I going to get to do that?' Because ever since I was old enough to reason I knew I was going to be an actor. I used to always apologize about it. I'd say, 'I know it sounds sloppy but people were born to do things and I was born to be an actor.' And then, just recently, someone did my astrological chart and said, 'You were born to be an actor.' So I knew I was going to be an actor, although I have no idea where it came from because there's no theatrical background in my family.

"My parents didn't want me to go into the theater. I was to be a diplomat—something my father never attained as much as he wanted to —or take over my father's business."

Perhaps it was because Winkler père objected to his offspring's show business ambitions that he enrolled him at an all-boy's school in New York when Henry began eighth grade. Henry remembers the motivation as a better education, so it is ironic that he began his acting career at McBurney School for Boys, appearing in school plays as long as his grades allowed it.

"I played *Billy Budd* by Herman Melville. I couldn't believe it when I got the part.

"See," he offers in a serious tone, "I wasn't a very good student in school. I wasn't good because I had a lot of pressure to be a good student from home, so I went the other way. I was always told how bright I was but how I wasn't meeting my potential, which is what everybody hears.

"Anyway, I got the main part, Billy Budd, and I couldn't believe it. I got it over better students. Everyone was telling me *they* were going to get it, how much better *they* were, and I was scared. But when I got it, it was a big thrill. Oh God, I loved it. I went out and bought a pair of black desert boots and wore them to school because that's what I was going to wear with my white sailor outfit in the play. I went over those lines and I rehearsed it and rehearsed it. It was my first major event in the theater, I guess, and I didn't do many plays after that.

"See, I got that role in the school play from an audition. I was in the Thespian Club, but since I wasn't a very good student I wasn't able to do very many plays. I lost out on a lot of roles because you had to maintain a certain grade average, which I didn't do.

"So, the next play I did was in the eleventh grade, *Of Thee I Sing*. I did a Christmas play before that, but the next big thing after *Billy Budd* was this one and I had to join the Glee Club for it. Well, I don't sing. When the Glee Club went to the Pan Am Building to perform at Christmas, there they were, all singing, and there I was, just mouthing it.

"On the other hand, I was a very good dancer. I won a lot of contests at the different school dances we threw. I think dancing is the second greatest physical action a human being can do," he explains, avoiding mention of the first.

"I never took formal lessons. I guess I have a lot of style but not the technique. I taught myself the Russian Kazatsky and I went to see the film version of *West Side Story* thirteen times and choreographed it in my room. See, my parents didn't want me to take dancing lessons. Actually, they didn't want me to have anything to do with the theatrical profession. As I said, my father's wish was for me to take over the family business."

In 1958 Henry was sent to study in Switzerland for four months. "That was my father's decision," he says. Mr. Winkler was providing his son with the well-rounded education he'd need as a successful businessman.

"It was a great experience, though," Henry remembers. "There were some Americans there, but most of the people were the crème of Europe and the Middle East. I studied with a kid named Salom; we were in the same boat crew. He was the Sheik of Kuwait's son. One fourth of all the world's oil comes from Kuwait, and at that time there wasn't this whole big barrier, so we had a great time together, a great time.

"The funniest thing happened on the day I left. I lived at the school, and each morning they used to wake us up with a bell. Well, on the last day, three others guys and I took the bell and hid it. They wouldn't let us leave the place until we found it. Miraculously, that bell was found very fast.

"Then there was the money. My parents had sent me money for any overweight luggage because I was going to meet them in Holland. So I dressed up in three layers of clothes and I hung all the souvenirs I'd collected on my belt, put them in my pockets, put them everywhere, so my suitcase had literally nothing in it. I saved all the money, spent it later in Holland."

The four months of elegant education did little for Henry's business interest. He was still hung up on acting.

"Everyone knew I wanted to be an actor," he explains, referring to his classmates at Mc-Burney. "See, everyone in my high school was bright and they all wanted to go to Princeton. Everyone was into wanting to be a preppy. I was into wanting to be an actor, so like I was the clown of the class, which is not always the best position to take, but that's what I did.

"I was also ultra-sensitive," he adds quickly. "I gave too much power away in my youth. I was always bowing to everybody else, and I would come back after summer vacations and I'd say, 'Okay guys, I've changed. I'm cool now. I'm all right now.' And I'd still be the brunt of the jokes. I was always able to be baited, and that was very painful to me because I never thought that I was good enough. I never thought that I was anything. For a long time I thought I was stupid, which was very painful."

On the other hand, school had some bright moments. Jerry Love, one of Henry's closest friends at McBurney's (the two boys were bar mitzvahed together in 1958) was one of them.

"Jerry and I would carry on something terrible on the bus enroute to school," Henry says. "At Christmas we would have everybody singing Christmas songs and Hanukah songs on the bus. We would just get up in the aisles and talk to everybody and we would have a seat in between us that was empty and if somebody started to sit down we'd go, 'Hold it! You were going to sit on our horse, George.' And we would have people laughing and talking to each other.

"One day I got on the bus during final exams and I was late. So I stood up on the Broadway bus and I said, 'Look, does anybody have to get off from between 78th Street and 63rd?' Nobody said they did, so I said, 'Okay, look, just understand this. I'm the future of America, and I'm taking my final exams and I've got to pass them to get out of that school, so is it okay if we just shoot down because I'm late?' And the bus went right down without stopping and I got there on time."

On the subject of girls, Henry says: "Well, even though I went to an all boys' school, we had sister schools, so there were always plenty of girls around. But I didn't really have a lot of girl friends.

"See, what would happen is that I would go to these temple dances and high-school dances and I was so needful, I had such a big need, that I would become a social butterfly. It was impossible for me to take a date to one of these things because I would just leave her and walk around, talk and deal with everybody. I'd just get into everything that was happening and my date would be left alone, which is a real drag.

"And then I'd have this great guilt. I would objectively see what I'd done. So no matter what I did during the week before I took the girl out, I'd prepare myself. Like I'd say, 'Okay you're going to be with her and you're going to take her around.' But when I walked into that place with all those people, something took me over and I was just off and running, flying to every section of that room. It made me crazy, because I also understood what I was doing. I understood that I was leaving the girl alone, but I had to entertain people.

"So I dated, but I didn't have girl friends in the true sense of the word. Additionally, I couldn't go out a lot because I didn't do well in school so I would be grounded for six weeks at a time at home.

"I didn't graduate from high school with all my classmates because I failed geometry. I had to take it over during the summer in order to have enough credits to graduate. See," he says, "I lost my virginity and passed geometry in the same summer.

"I was shattered at the time because I couldn't graduate with my classmates, but I had made the bed so I had to lie in it. I repeat, I wasn't a good student in high school."

Thinking back on it, Henry realizes that he created a lot of his own scholastic problems. But when he was young, he felt plagued by his father's constant pressure to do well, to excel academically.

"Almost everything my father did with us kids was some kind of educational project. He took me to New Brunswick, Canada, to a lumbermill with my friend Jerry Love in our senior year of high school, and we always had to figure out the mileage from town-to-town. That was our job. When we went to Europe the last time, we took an overnight train to Canada first so we could go through the St. Lawrence Seaway since it had just opened. My father felt it would be an educational experience along with travel."

CHAPTER 3

"Mrs. Winkler Is Henry's Best Press Agent"

Henry's parents, Harry Irving and Ilse Anna Maria Winkler, fled Berlin in 1939, for Holland. Harry had lost two brothers, and Ilse had lost her only brother before they managed to escape Hitler's Germany. Their families gone, their homes overrun, their future in their homeland destroyed, the Winklers had only their wits, strength, and intelligence to survive. From Holland, which was also occupied by the Nazis, Harry and Ilse Winkler made their way to America. A well-educated man, Harry Winkler had held citizenships in both Germany and Hungary and so was able to manage entry into the United States.

In numerous stories written about the couple's famous son, there have been references to the family's wealth. But in reality the Winklers arrived in New York so poor that Harry had to hock what family jewelry he had been able to smuggle out of Germany. Settling into their new world, the Winklers had their first child in 1942: a daughter, Beatrice Harriet. Three years later, on October 30, 1945, their second child and only son, Henry, was born in New York's West Side Hospital.

The elder Winklers still live in the apartment that was Henry's childhood home, although its location has been discovered by numerous over-zealous fans, causing them occasional inconvenience. Except for changing their phone number, they lead their old, familiar lives. They remain active in their own business interests and civic affairs, and spend as much time as they can with their granddaughters from Beatrice's marriage. If they're flattered by the recognition their son has attained and the attention that it has brought them, their lifestyle belies it.

A family friend describes the Winklers this way:

"Mrs. Winkler is an attractive, middle-aged, heavily accented woman. She can seem tough and cold when you first meet her, but quite warm and a real charmer when you get to know her. She has volumes of every word that has ever been written by or about Henry and will even show you his bar mitzvah album with pride. A friend of his told me that at one of his earliest performances she came with a box of cookies and gave one to anyone who said something nice about his acting.

"Henry definitely gets most of his charm from his father—who is also quite attractive. He's got that same wonderful talent that Henry does—to instantly make people comfortable. Even if there are fifty other people in the room, when he talks to you, it is as if they aren't there.

"Henry's parents were not in favor of his becoming an actor. His father, who is in the international lumber business and quite successful, naturally wanted him to go into the family business. It's a typical Jewish family—an obviously strong-willed mother, and both parents dedicated to their two children.

"Mrs. Winkler is Henry's best press agent and seems to be enjoying her new celebrity status. Although it took her a while to get used to the **idea** of her son being an actor, she claims that all her reservations were eliminated once she saw Henry on stage. They are incredibly proud of him, and they are particularly proud that he has changed so little since becoming a star.

"Henry still stays at their house when he comes to New York (as opposed to a fancy hotel that he can well afford), which is the same apartment Henry grew up in. It's a very homey place and probably furnished the same way it has been for years. It's full of pictures of the family, and one wall has an ad from the *Lords of Flatbush*, Henry's *TV Guide* feature, and the *Crawdaddy* cover.

"Henry always stops to chat with the neighbors and finds time to go to the synagogue with his father. Henry's strong sense of his Jewish identity is something they are very proud of. It's a very tight family. Some months ago Henry flew into New York for the weekend to surprise his sister on her birthday.

"Henry has always been a charmer, and the girls were after him for years. Ilse says that she can't remember the first girl that he ever brought home, but the house was always full of Henry's friends—both male and female. She glows about him constantly and tells about the mail that comes to her house for him. She recalled to me

once that there was a girl—from Florida, I think
—who has been writing him every day for a
year—even sent roses on his birthday. She's not
quite sure what the whole cult trip is about but
is now beginning to understand the enormity
of Henry's success. Like any Jewish mother,
though, all she wants is for everyone to like
Henry.

"She says that she 'could rent all of Madison
Square Garden to have a dinner for all the family
and friends who want to see Henry.' He calls
his mother faithfully every Sunday night, and
when he's traveling, she always knows where to
reach him. He checks in with his sister Beatrice
and her children regularly too.

"His mother never misses his show (in New
York it's on in reruns every day at 11:30 A.M.).
I remember some months ago, I got a message
to call Mrs. Winkler. I realized it was the hospital where Mr. Winkler had had a cataract
operation the day before. I had difficulty hearing
her until she turned down the television set. She
had been watching reruns of *Happy Days*. As
she once told me, 'If God forbid, someone died
on a Tuesday night, I guess I'd have to catch it
in reruns.'"

CHAPTER 4

"Do You Think Henry Has Talent?"

Leo Nickole, chairman of the Theatre Education Department at Emerson College, which Henry Winkler had attended for four years, remembers meeting Henry's mother and father "during one of the musicals he was doing here; I think it was *Carnival*. His parents are very European in their approach, as they should be. They said to me, 'He wanted to come here, fine, but we really want him to go into business.' They kept asking, 'Do you think Henry has talent?' And I'd tell them that he's what I'd call a very presentational performer, and that 'he must be given the opportunity to work it out.'"

Henry's tenure at Emerson didn't begin very promisingly. "I was in a kind of fog," he says, "trying to acclimate myself to being an adult. I nearly flunked out during my first year. I couldn't get with it."

What saved him was a course in child psychology, a subject inspired by his interest in kids.

"I was in high school when I went to work at the Yorkville Youth Center, working with so-called underprivileged kids after the school day was finished. I walked in as an assistant and walked out as the head counselor for an entire school. I really loved it. I mean I love children, I love their potential and I love to be with them.

"Well, that rapport with young people carried over into college, and that's one of the reasons I studied child psychology. The other reason was because I knew I'd never make it as an actor.

"During my freshman year in college and the following summer I counseled in camps and at the school. I took a lot of new students on tours around Emerson for the administration office. I would take them around and be very charming so the administration would think I was a nice guy and let me back for another year. I started doing very well in my sophomore year because I suddenly realized why I was there and why I wanted to be there.

"Also in my sophomore year I got into a fraternity, Alpha Pi Theta, which I really enjoyed. I was really rah, rah in college. I still am! I mean I liked the whole thing of college so I got into this fraternity, but I had such a loud mouth I would have to drop for push-ups all the time. I had to let out my shirts because my arms grew. I was such a wise guy I kept dropping for a hundred push-ups. 'All right, Winkler, drop for a hundred.'

"I remember," he says with a fond grin, "the time I had to hitchhike to a small Canadian town about eighty miles outside of Ottawa. I had to hitchhike there on my birthday as part of our initiation. We had to wear pajamas outside our clothing, and it was cold. We had to wear a straw hat and carry a red brick painted in gold with two-inch high letters, 'Alpha Pi Theta.' And we had no money. It was one thousand, five hundred and thirty-eight miles round trip.

There were three of us, and I talked us into food three times a day."

It was also during his sophomore year that Henry fell in love. "Her name was Susan." She had dark hair with a blonde streak in the front. I want to tell you! I lived down the block from her. I saw her about twenty-four hours a day. I wrote her one hundred and fifty letters trying to put into words exactly what it was I felt for her. I would make phone calls by dropping in a nickel and hitting the coin return, which would make the connection. And sometimes when we had an argument I had to call her back and my rhythm was off and I wouldn't make the connection when I hit the phone.

"I'd hit that phone so many times my thumb would swell up, grow out to here," he says with a gesture several inches beyond his hand. "And I'd not have another nickel so I'd have to go borrow money. Oh it was tragic," he grins. "And then I'd be on the toilet because I had diarrhea."

The romance with Susan was interrupted during the summer of Henry's junior year. His father sent him to Germany in still another effort to detour the kid's theatrical pursuits.

"My father and I recreated all the great wars of history," he has said frequently during interviews when mentioning his parents' reaction to his interest in acting. "My mother was more subtle. She'd fix breakfast for me—eggs, toast and guilt."

Nevertheless, his parents acknowledged their son's passion by taking him to a review called *America, America* in Holland, and to the German theatre, the ballet, and the opera.

But this trip to Germany contained nothing artistic. Henry was being sent on a tour of lumbermills.

"My father wanted me to learn his business from the bottom up, and so I worked in a lumbermill over there. I had a great time, even wrote seventy-one songs. I worked at a machine that made so much noise all anyone could see was me mouthing the words. They couldn't hear me, so I sung at the top of my lungs writing to Susie—I wrote her seventy-one love songs. I mailed some of them to her, most of them in fact, because this was just my way of getting out the pain of missing her."

Little did Henry know that his efforts were in vain. "These are such sad stories," he says mockingly. "I would call her from Germany too. I didn't eat. I saved up all my money and I'd call her at least once a week and I'd write her two letters a day because I missed her so much."

But the romance came to an abrupt end when Henry returned to Emerson.

"I drove up to Boston, walked into the girls' dormitory, and she was walking out with another guy. So we broke up and then I met this wonderful girl, Jennifer, who was my second great love in college.

"So many of the girls I dated in college were just dates, but Jennifer was an angel. She was wonderful, but I was really emotionally immature. Having a relationship and knowing what a relationship is all about are two different things, so that didn't last long."

Scholastically, Henry's junior year was also on a downswing. He was kicked out of acting class for being consistently late. He talked his way back in—was kicked out once more—then talked his way back in again. This was not exactly conducive to getting great grades.

Leo Nickole, the Emerson professor who worked with Henry in numerous college productions, says: "I do remember that he was never an outstanding scholastic student, as Henry will tell you himself. But what he did have is what a lot of students need. He had a tremendous amount of personal push. He had a determination that I had not seen in students in many, many years. His first year, for example, he found that he could work very well as a dancer. Now his first show with us, I believe, was in the dancing chorus of *Finian's Rainbow*. I liked his work very much because he was very much a presentational actor—I mean he radiated beyond the footlights. Well, that musical occurred near the end of his freshman year, and I think this inspired him to continue, to return to Emerson his second year."

Of course, it was during his first year at college that Henry almost dropped out of school because of poor grades. On his return, Leo Nickole remembers him appearing in *Carnival*, "as a dancer, primarily.

"That same year he joined Alpha Pi Theta fraternity, and this is where Henry started really working very well with the other students. Alpha Pi Theta," Nickole explains, "has the best of the men on campus. Henry started relating socially there dating and things of that sort. He was a very well-liked student.

"It was in his junior year, though," Nickole continues, "that he started working in more serious drama. He did another musical, *Fantastick's,* and he was wonderful in that. Then he went into a serious study of drama, and I think that's when he really found himself theatrically. Once he broke that barrier he went straight ahead. He performed *Peer Gynt*, for example, and he also appeared in a new play at the time, *Donner*. Both of these plays were directed by Thomas Haas, who was his acting teacher here his last two years. He received a tremendous amount of help from Dr. Haas, and those two roles were probably the most influential ones he had while at Emerson."

It was Haas's class. Leo Nickole remembers,

from which Henry was dismissed during his junior year.

"Tom Haas was the type of teacher who believed in tremendous discipline. That meant that if the class started at three o'clock you didn't arrive at five minutes past three, you got there early and you waited. It's a matter of trying to teach the student discipline, that's the whole idea, and it was in Tom Hass's classes that Henry had to deal a lot with that disciplined technique."

Nickole describes young Henry as a "diamond in the rough" type of actor. "Once he grasped something, his personality was able to convey this to an audience very nicely. But he worked. God, that boy worked! At times he felt he might not be intellectually on a par with the rest of the students, but that didn't hold him back at all. He worked so hard to make up that difference. He was so determined to know everything there is to know, whether it be his work with his voice, his work with his body, or his work with his scenes.

"I kept telling him back in those early days that I thought he would be a very good musical-comedy personality. What's strange is that the role he does now is really musical-comedy. Henry's *Peer Gynt* was outstanding, primarily because he became so theatricalized. I personally did not like his *Donner* because it was an older character. But I loved his *Peer Gynt* and I loved the work he did when he dealt with lighter characterizations. That's why his Fonzie is so good. And yet, you know," Nickole says with a laugh, "I saw his Fonzie when he was doing *Finian's Rainbow!*"

CHAPTER 5

"... I Was Always
Very Emotional"

Henry remembers his senior year at Emerson with a mixture of sorrow and pride. "I thought I was pulling the wool over everybody's eyes when in fact I had the wool over my own eyes. I was going through an identity crisis. I was going to graduate and didn't know if I was ever going to make it as an actor. I didn't know what was going to happen, and I really shook. I mean, I stayed a lot by myself. I became anti-social. I was obsessed with the future. I figured if I wasn't an actor, I'd be a child psychologist— this is only a year before I graduated! I always lived months and years ahead of myself. I was never in the moment. I was always way ahead, and I was always very emotional."

Most of that emotion was reflected in Henry's work on stage. Despite his self-doubts, he was doing plays with the Children's Story Theatre, earning $12 a performance, as well as acting in numerous college productions. Two of those put him on the map as an outstanding theatrical student.

"I pulled off a coup my senior year," he says. "I got the two largest parts: *Peer Gynt* by Ibsen, and *Donner* by Robert Murray, a three-hour epic about the Donner Pass in 1864. I got both parts, but at that time I still wasn't together so I didn't realize until years later that I never even knew my lines. I got an award for the most sensitive translation of Ibsen—and I made it up!

"*Peer Gynt* was written in the 1800s, and I

was saying, 'I had the Khrushchev on my knees.' I mean, I'd say whatever came to my mind just to fill up the space. I had monologues four pages long, and I didn't know the lines so I made them up!"

Nevertheless Henry was listed in *Who's Who In American Colleges and Universities;* he was elected Kappa Gamma Chi's (a sorority) "Sweetheart," an honor given at the end of each school year; he was named Most Outstanding Person by a professional sorority, and he was named Most Outstanding Performer for his four years of theatrical study.

Such credentials brought Henry invitations from both the Yale School of Drama and the New York University School of Drama.

"Both of them are reputable," Henry says, "but I chose Yale. In fact, when they called me and asked if I'd like to act at Yale I said yes, hung up the phone, fell off the couch, ran to the window, and yelled to Boston, 'I got into Yale!' Then I ran out of my place to tell everybody and it cost me $12 because I left my keys inside and had to hire a locksmith."

Henry spent three years at Yale where he was awarded a Master of Fine Arts degree. He also spent a year and a half with the professional Yale Repertory Company.

"That was a terrific experience," he says, "but I still was so insecure. Twenty-five actors started and eleven finished. The instructors kept saying, 'A lot of you are not going to finish,' and I figured, 'Well, I'll just go pack my bags because I know I'm going to be one of those.' I cried myself to sleep worrying about that.

"But what happened was that I did a lot of plays. From 1967 to 1971 I did over sixty stage plays. Then, during my senior year at Yale, my last year, I went to Chicago for the TCG's, which is Theatre Communications Group. Thirty-nine actors every half year go there and audition for all the repertory companies in the country, and out of fourteen theaters I got about ten offers. One of them was from Yale's Repertory Company, so I went back to Yale and they offered me a job. Now, out of those eleven survivors in the Yale School of Drama, only three of us were asked right into the company and I was one of them.

"So we started in the summer at the John Drew Theatre in East Hampton, Long Island, and it was a very ambivalent time for me because here I am getting paid and I'm saying, 'Am I worth it? Do I have the talent to actually be paid for what I want to do?' All that stuff, so that kind of colored my performances a lot. Yet, some of the best reviews I ever got were during that first summer."

Henry received high critical acclaim as the original Grossbart in Philip Roth's *Defender of the Faith,* but he also remembers his lone "bad" review.

"My very first review was good," he admits. "They compared me to a young Dustin Hoffman. The one bad review I got was when we did *The Revenger's Tragedy* and I played a 16-year-old rapist. They said, 'He's got a New York accent.' But that was it. I was really lucky."

Carmen de Lavallade, the celebrated dancer and actress who was one of Henry's instructors at Yale, remembers him as being much more than lucky; he was talented.

"I act in the company at Yale," she explains, "but I'm also the person who teaches movement for actors. I don't like to use the word 'dance,' because what I teach actors is a little different. Henry was in my class, and I worked with him in some of the shows we did here at Yale. A particular one was *The Seven Deadly Sins;* we were partners in that one. He was an excellent partner. We happened to be working on a really steep, raked stage and it was very precarious, but Henry was just fantastic. He was very strong. I'm relatively tall, but he was so together and he moved so well he was just wonderful to work with. We had one of those moments in the play when I'd take off on a turn or something and he had to be there on a certain count because if he wasn't that was the end of me. But he was always exactly on time.

"And then once in East Hampton we were doing some Phillip Roth plays, and I played Henry's Jewish mother. In fact, his own mother taught me the Friday night ceremony with the candles for the play. It was great fun."

She recalls vividly that "Henry didn't have very much faith in himself. I was constantly trying to encourage him because people need that when they're performing. And, oh goodness, he was terrible about getting discouraged. I used to get angry with him. I'd have to push him a little bit because he'd get mad at himself and then he'd get discouraged. He was a perfectionist, at least I personally thought so, in his work and in my classes. He came to them regularly and he worked very hard. And like I said, when I performed with him and he was required to be in a certain position on stage at a particular moment he was always where he was supposed to be."

As for her former student's current success, she says: "It must be a frightening as well as a wonderful experience to have happen what's happened to Henry. It's difficult to keep one's head on one's shoulders. He came here recently and he spoke to the students. He really spoke well and everybody was surprised. 'Oh Henry hasn't changed.' I kept telling them, 'Of course, he hasn't changed. I saw Henry in California and he hasn't changed a lick.'

"Now, that's rather hard to believe of a person who has had that much success, but it's really true. When he spoke to the students he was so down to earth, and he wasn't afraid to answer their questions or give his opinions, even if they happened to be contrary to someone else's. He gave very good reasons why he thought what he did and I think the students really got a lot out of it. They learned a lot and were very impressed with his whole attitude, his ideas. The lovely thing is that what he learned here he's using now. He is using his craft and he encouraged the students to use their's in their work. He is today what he was when he was a student himself. I always found him to be a very sensitive and very fine person, and he's still that today. It's really true—he hasn't changed."

He may not have changed personally, but the way he lives now is quite different from the good old days at Yale.

"For two years I lived in a kind of commune," he says. "Those were two of the best years I've ever had in a living situation. I lived in a house on the beach in New Haven, Connecticut, sharing it with six people. I was the only actor. Guys and girls lived together, but everybody had his own bedroom and own social life. And everybody had his own chores. Mine was to clean the bathrooms, but I didn't mind at all. It was a very civilized way to live, very much like a family.

"Like, if somebody had a birthday, we would have a party. The girls made a cake and the boys put on a show. We'd pretend we were rock stars and we'd put on a record album on the stereo and we'd grab parts of the vacuum cleaner and pretend they were instruments. I was either the drummer or the lead singer. The girls would sit on the stairs watching the performance, cheering and yelling. We just had the greatest of times. Playing together. Working together."

But emotionally satisfying as the situation was, Henry realized he had to move on to other experiences. "I knew I had to grow" he remembers. "I was getting too comfortable. I was having a great time though, and I got a ten dollar a week raise to go to the Arena Theatre in Washington, D.C., a good place. But after three weeks of rehearsal on the first play I got fired. The producer told me it was the director. The director told me it was the playwright, and the playwright told me he had nothing to do with it. It didn't matter, I was out of work."

CHAPTER 6

"The Biggest Commercial I Ever Did Was for Close-Up Toothpaste"

Henry had saved some some money, and that plus his severence pay from the Arena Theatre enabled him to rent a small apartment in New York's Greenwich Village for a month. He figured he'd find some kind of work during his first thirty days to pay for the second month. The one thing he'd never do was return home to live or ask his father for money. Although the Winklears appeared to accept the inevitable—that Henry was going to continue to act—it was obvious that the pressures would return if he was unable to provide for himself.

So he had to find a job, but not just any job and especially not one that required him to work nights. Since all plays were presented in the evening, Henry had to be free for a stage role, when or if one materialized. So he went to work as a travel agent during the day and did free shows at night. Each morning, before showing up at the office, he scrutinized the list of auditions. Nothing—or at least very little was coming his way in the theater. So unless he was willing to make the travel agency his life's work, he had to find other places to be an actor.

"I started doing commercials because I couldn't get arrested elsewhere," he says. "I did thirty commercials. I got real good at getting them. In fact, I got to the point where I could get two a day, all class-A television commercials. That was great because it allowed me to do plays at night for free."

It also allowed him to quit his travel agent job six weeks after his arrival in New York.

"I've been self-sufficient, really, since I got out of graduate school. As an actor, I've only been out of work for six weeks at a time. The commercials kept me alive for a year and a half, and I was able to do plays for weeks at a time in between commercials.

"In fact, there was one time during a three week period when I was doing *MacBeth* and *Dark Lady of the Sonnet,* by Shaw, at the same time. When I finished the first performance of *MacBeth* I'd run to the other theater and do that performance and then go back and do the late night performance of the first play. It was tiring but it was great—great training.

"But I did that at Yale too. I mean, I would rehearse a play in the afternoon, maybe do a student play after that, and then do still another play after that one."

Such a schedule didn't come without a price. "I contracted walking pneumonia when I was at Yale," Henry says. "I was doing a play with the Children's Theatre, I'd do two performances a day, then the rest of the cast would take me home and I would faint dead out because I was acting while I had pneumonia. I couldn't walk, couldn't breathe, but I was perfectly well when I acted."

In New York the problems were psychological, not physical.

"The biggest commercial I ever did was for Close-Up toothpaste," he says. "When I went in for the interview there were nothing but models, all models in the reception room with me. I looked around and almost freaked out. I said, 'Why did my agent send me here? Look at all these beautiful people,' And there's me sitting in the middle. They all had their Dunhill lighters and their Dunhill leather this and that and I'm sitting there like a shmuck!

"So anyway," Henry says with a chuckle, "I walked into the room and I said, 'Henry, you've got to do what you've got to do.' I learned a very important lesson at that interview. I thought, 'You are who you are. You give them what you've got, and if it's not good enough you go somewhere else.

"Still, when I was sitting there, one of the agency bigshots walked up to me. Now you must realize they made me smile a lot, you know, every other minute, 'Smile, please,' to see your teeth. And so this guy walks up and he says, 'You know you have spinach in your teeth?' And I said, 'Sir, you know that's not true. Why don't you just go over there and sit down!'

"Well I thought I'd blown the job, but I got it and it made me the most money I ever earned from a commercial."

How did he discover the lucrative world of commercials? Like most people, via an agent. Henry's help came from "Tina Jacobsen, a very important influence in my life. She was working for another agency at the time, and I sat down to visit with her and never got up. She got me every commercial I did. Then, when she started her own agency, I actually picked up the files at her old office and carried them to her new office. We've been together ever since. I don't do commercials anymore but I'm still with the agency. If I ever have to do commercials again, I will only do them through Tina and Jackie Wilder. They are the greatest.

"Now my theatrical agent is a different person. The girl I was dating, a dancer, had an agent she introduced me to. In fact, her agent signed me sight unseen. I mean, she'd never seen me work, but we met and Joan Scott signed me and I've been with her since the beginning of my career."

But before Joan entered his life, Henry continued with the commercials. He starred for products like Schick Injector Blades and the A&P, roles which led to such NET (public television) programs as *The Great American Dream Machine* and *Masquerade*.

Through new friends Henry had made since his arrival in New York, he also became part of a successful improvisational group called *Off The Wall*. "I didn't put it together myself as has been reported," Henry says. "My best friend at that time, Mark Flannigan, whom I've worked with as an actor in a lot of pieces, got together with me, Mark Lano, Joan Astro, and Mickey Flacks and we organized *Off The Wall*. It presented a jaundiced view of living in New York. We wrote our own material and staged our own shows, pretty successfully. Mark eventually took it over, and I think he still has the group, but there are very few of the original members in it." *Off The Wall* was a very important part of Henry's life at the time. A black-and-white poster advertising the group hangs in his place even today.

The exposure on off-Broadway along with the improvisations presented through *Off The Wall* provided an ideal showcase for Henry, enabling him to gain the lead role in *Ubu Roi*, another off-Broadway production. It was the fall of 1972. A short time later he got his first movie role in *The Lords of Flatbush*.

CHAPTER 7

"Out of the Blue Came Lords of Flatbush"

Henry and Mark Lano were inseparable during their years in New York. Not only did they work together in *Off the Wall,* they were close personal friends, buddies, anxious to help each other succeed.

"Mark and I were walking down the street one day," Henry remembers, "when out of the blue he said, 'Have you heard about this movie, *Lords of Flatbush?'* I said no, and Mark told me what he knew about it. It sounded interesting, so my agent, Joan, called Marty Davidson, who was the director of the film, and I went and auditioned a couple of days later from one o'clock until five. Finally, they asked me, at five o'clock, if I wanted to do it. I said yes.

"It was a low-budget film." The producers were really hard up for money.

"I was doing *Lords of Flatbush* from six in the morning until around eight at night. Then, from nine to ten P.M. I was rehearsing Story Theatre—a great experience, one of the best things I ever did in New York. Then later that night I'd inevitably find myself meeting with the group *(Off The Wall)* and we'd write together. Then I'd be up at six A.M. to report to work for the movie."

Lords had a small cast of young unknown actors, although a number of them—Henry, of course, Susan Blakely of *Rich Man, Poor Man*— have since gone on to bigger things. The film centered on the romantic escapades of two young Brooklyn toughs—Chico Tyrell, played by Perry King, (remember him in *Mandingo, Lipstick*?) and Stanley Rosiello, played by Sylvester Stallone (starring in the movie *Rocky*). Henry's role of Butchey was a supporting one.

But Henry played Butchey as a true three-dimensional character. He wasn't just a tough member of the gang, he was an artist with a promising future—providing he decided to pursue that future. Of all the Lords, only Butchey appeared to have any ambition or any intelligence. As a result, the owner of the candy store where the Lords hung out would wait until the other gang members left, then encourage Butchey to forget about the gang and pursue his artistic talents. Butchey would listen carefully for a few moments, then curl his lip, thrust his thumbs in his pockets, and dismiss the suggestion. Butchey was already somebody, he already had prestige—he belonged to the *Lords of Flatbush*.

Playboy Magazine gave the film a fine review, calling it "realistically photographed and explosively funny, an honest and downbeat recollection of what it was like to be growing up in the 50's."

Reviewer Don Glut went on to say: "As I watched the film I couldn't help but recall how seriously I and my friends once took the very things that now seem to be so humorous in the *Lords of Flatbush*. Henry Winkler and the other actors played their roles with that same sobriety, and let the humor emerge accordingly."

When Columbia Pictures first released the film, it fared only moderately at the box office. Unlike *American Graffiti*, which also dealt with the 1950s, it was not an immediate hit. Gradually, however, by word-of-mouth, audiences discovered the *Lords,* and it skyrocketed to a box office gross of $2 million in New York alone. More recently, with Henry's emergence on *Happy Days,* its television presentation was also a super success.

In between his work on *Lords* and various other projects, Henry found time for his Broadway debut, in *42 Seconds From Broadway.* "We opened in February," he says, "and closed on March 11th. Fortunately, in June of '73 I got *Crazy Joe.*"

Crazy Joe was one of a long line of Mafia movies. It was not one of the successful ones, even though it did boast a solid cast in Peter Boyle (in the title role), Paula Prentiss, Eli Wallach, Fred Williamson. And of course Henry Winkler. Loosely modeled on Brooklyn's Joey Gallo, the film featured Henry as "Crazy Joe's most solid supporter, a soldier in the gang wars who fought with Joe and didn't desert him when he was in prison," Henry explains.

As Mannie, Henry had a number of meaty dramatic scenes. He was at Joe's side during many of the bloody gang fights, and at one point he was the one who found the severed hand of a fellow gang member protruding from a cardboard box filled with cement—a "warning" from a rival faction. Outfitted in a suit, tie, and mustache, it was hard to recognize Henry Winkler, The Fonz, in Mannie, the hood.

Because the film was so violent—and because Henry's role involved him in most of the gangland war scenes—much of Henry Winkler is edited out of *Crazy Joe* when the film is shown on television. Despite this, and despite the movie's copious lack of box office and critical success, Henry calls *Crazy Joe* an "important film" in his acting career.

"It placed me in a different league because of the stars who were in it. Even if I was always in the shadow of these people—and rightly so—the movie projected me in an entirely different light than the *Lords* did."

It also convinced his agent that it was time for Henry to leave New York for Hollywood, where not only films but also television roles were much more available. Henry didn't want to leave. "Every day for two weeks my agent would say, 'It's time for you to go.' And I'd say, 'No.'"

He kept thinking: "What are they going to want with a short Jewish kid in Hollywood?"

Henry Winkler as "Fonzie"—the ultimate in cool.

Off-screen, Henry makes a long phone call to a friend from the living room of his Hollywood apartment.

Henry relaxing beneath a Mexican wall hanging in his bedroom.

Loosening up his pitching arm by the side of his backyard pool.

At a recent celebrity basketball game, Winkler jokes with fellow actor James Caan.

Yani Begakis

Jamie Lynn Bauer, one of the regulars on ABC-TV's "The Young and the Restless," was Henry's steady for six months. Now they both say they're just "good friends."

On Malibu Beach, he gets some time to read and rel[e] by himself. He says, "The ocean is like a big magnet . . it draws me to it."

**Henry Franklin Winkler's Bio
for the Yale Rep's production of
Gogol's "The Inspector General" in 1970.**

HENRY FRANKLIN WINKLER (Pyotr Ivanovich Dobchinsky)
Mr. Winkler, '70, received his B.A. from Emerson College where
he studied theatre arts and psychology. As an undergraduate he
played the title role in **Peer Gynt** and the Indian in **The Fan-
tasticks**, as well as dancing in several musicals. For two years
Mr. Winkler worked in professional children's theatre, playing the
title role in **The Brave Little Tailor** with the Children's Hour
Players. He appeared in **The American Pig** at the New York
Shakespeare Festival's Public Theatre, and in several productions
with the New Haven Free Theatre. Mr. Winkler was featured in last
year's production of **They Told Me That You Came This Way,**
and was a member of the chorus in **Bacchae.** He has appeared in
numerous revues and sketches at the Yale Cabaret, including the
recent **Cocaloony, Tennessee,** and recently played Hamm in the
Studio Theatre production of Beckett's **Endgame.** Mr. Winkler was
also seen in three Workshop Series productions: **The White Devil,
Sweeney/Hughie,** and **The Physicists,** in which he played Ernst
Heinrich Ernesti ("Einstein").

Sean Kernan

During the Yale Rep's 1969-70 season, he played the part
of Pyotr Ivanovich Dobchinsky in Gogol's play *The Inspector General.*

Henry appeared with Joan Pape in the 1970 Yale Repertory Theatre production of Moliere's Don Juan.

The four "Lords of Flatbush" slouch for a group portrait. (From left: Paul Mace, Sylvester Stallone, Henry Winkler, Perry King)

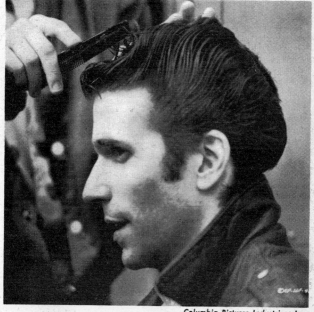

Henry gets his first D.A. haircut for his role in "The Lords of Flatbush."

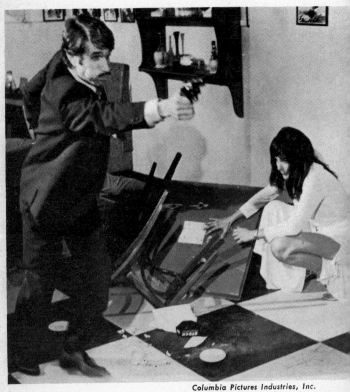

"Crazy Joe's" girlfriend (Paula Prentiss) crouches in terror while Joe's bodyguard Mannie (Henry Winkler) tries to gun down mob killers.

In another scene from "Crazy Joe," Willy (Fred Williamson) makes Mannie an offer he can't refuse.

Globe Photos

The cast and crew of "Happy Days" sometimes get together for a friendly softball game—this is "Fonzie's" turn at bat.

Fonzie tries to put some muscle into his new job as an arbitrator between rival gangs in this episode from "Happy Days."

The "Happy Days" big four. From left to right, Ralph Malph (Donny Most), Arthur Fonzarelli—better known as "The Fonz" (Henry Winkler), Potsie Weber (Anson Williams), and Richie Cunningham (Ronnie Howard).

The Cunningham family (Ron Howard, Erin Moran, Mario
Ross, Tom Bosley) from "Happy Days."

Fonzie surprises Shirley (Cindy Williams), Richie and Laverne (Penny Marshall) by taking the stage for a singer who couldn't make it and belting out a song like a pro.

Globe Photos.

CHAPTER 8

"I Cried Myself to Sleep"

In his innermost heart he was convinced he'd made a horrible mistake. He'd had no idea how sprawling Los Angeles was, with its track homes, shopping centers, and industrial parks spread up, down, and around mountains. There was no subway, scarcely any buses, no theater district—just a never-ending snake of freeways filled with cars. His entire life was in the billfold in his hip pocket and the lone suitcase at his side.

"I had no guarantees for work, nothing," Henry says, recalling that painful September 18th in 1973. "I came out here with a thousand dollars and hope."

His first home in Hollywood was the apartment of a friend of his agent. For the first several nights he slept on the sofa, although he remembers that he actually got little sleep because he spent most of the time lying in the dark, listening to the constant rumble of a nearby freeway, and wondering what he'd done to his life.

"Eight days after I got out here," Henry says, "I cried myself to sleep. I was that scared and frustrated. Somebody said to me, 'You know, it's going to be very hard to sell you out here.' And I said, meekly, 'Well, everybody told me I should come here and now I'm told it's going to be hard to sell me.' I figured it was a thousand dollar, three thousand mile mistake that someone had made with my life!"

Despite his pessimism, by the end of his first

month he'd found a modest, furnished apartment, rented a car, and bought a city map. Actually, he was forced to move when his agent's friend acquired a roommate and Henry found himself sleeping in the apartment's bathroom.

In addition—and rather typically—seventeen days after he arrived in Hollywood, his "nerves shot, frustrated, and worried that I'd run out of money," he read for a role on *The Mary Tyler Moore Show*. He got it, portraying Valerie Harper's date.

"Valerie is one of my favorite women in the world," Henry says. "She is concerned, intelligent, talented. She has a phenomenal sense of humor. Time for everybody. And she's professional. I appreciate every one of those qualities. She's a very aware woman, very open. It's a pleasure to have had the opportunity to work with her."

He appeared opposite Valerie again a few years later, on her own series, *Rhoda*. He also acted in *The Bob Newhart Show* and in the pilot for *The Paul Sand Show,* all of them MTM Production programs. Henry calls MTM (owned by Mary Tyler Moore and her husband Grant Tinker) "fabulous. They're civilized, wonderful people, the crème de la crème, you know."

Henry made six appearances on MTM shows, jobs which established him as a working actor in Hollywood—but which also got him the reputation of being "difficult." In the *Newhart* episode, Henry didn't like his lines, found he couldn't get the director to change them, so he stormed off to one of the show's producers. The producer told him to play them any way he wanted to.

"That director hates me to this day," Henry says. Whether that's true or not, Henry's first year in Hollywood was a productive one, even if it was filled with continued doubt and frustration. He missed New York. He missed not seeing his parents when he wanted to. He missed his friends from *Off The Wall*.

"My career is here, the career that's changed my life, but I'd much rather be in New York," he says. "There is a certain vitality there, a wanting. That's the cultural center of the world. It is *the* city."

In an interview in *Crawdaddy* Magazine, he's said, "I'm fascinated by the people in New York. I'm intrigued by how we are, the way we are,— at least in the Western culture. There has got to be an easier way to relate. Long Island is a microcosm of that. There's this place called Martell's out here. It's a single's bar. And everybody, oh," he shrugged, "everybody who goes there is saying, 'I hate this bar. I am not really here. I don't come here.' But there they are! The chicks are just looking for a place to spend the weekend and the guys are just looking for the chicks." Then he talked about the museums, the theatres, the taxi cabs that make up New York's very special style—one he loves and misses.

Still, there is no going back. At least not now. Hollywood is where his future is. That's where Arthur Fonzarelli brings home the bread.

The original pilot of *Happy Days* was produced as a segment of the then popular series, *Love, American Style*. Only Ron Howard, Anson Williams, and Marion Ross of the current cast were in the show.

"Everyone thinks it's a spin-off from *American Graffiti*," Henry says, "but it's not." *Graffiti* helped the interest in the new pilot, but it came after *Days*.

"My character was something they added later because they thought they needed it when they were going into a series."

It wasn't easy for Henry to get the Fonzie role. He had moved from New York to Hollywood just three months earlier, and when his agent sent him to audition for the role he was convinced he'd never get it.

"I walked in with even longer hair than I have now," he recalls, "and I figured they wanted a big sharker for the part. The guy ahead of me had gone in with his hair greased and in a D.A. That guy was Mickey Dolenz of *The Monkees*. An established star was going in there and they didn't even know me! What chance did I have? I was thinking, 'I'm out of the running. I don't even know why I'm here, and I'm scared.'

"Then I walked in and I said, 'I really don't think I'm the guy you're looking for.' But Tom Miller, one of the show's executive producers, really had a lot of faith in me. The next day I read for ABC and I got the part. It was on my birthday."

Nevertheless, when Henry co-starred in the new pilot for the series The Fonz had a total of six lines. If Henry had doubts about doing the role previously, he had even more then.

"I didn't know if I wanted to do a series or not because you get locked in," he explains. "But also, I was trained to be an 'artist,' " he says mockingly. "I was trained to do 'theater,' " he adds in the same way.

"However, I had a long talk with the executive producer and I said, 'Look, I've got to make him a complete human being or I won't do it. He's got to be tough, but he still has got to have feelings. He's still affected by things.' And he said, 'Well, that's what we want,' and they've allowed me to do that."

Still, in the early episodes of the series The Fonz was merely a cycle-riding greaser, a hip-swiveling sex-symbol for the impressionable young girls at Arnold's, someone who was "cool" for the three younger stars of the series to admire. He was an immediate popular character, but he was kept on the edge of the show's plot, almost incidental to the real storyline.

Robert Hoffman, dialogue coach on the show,

has said: "Henry wanted to keep his lines small. He was creating Fonzie all along. He knew the impact of the character was drained if he talked too much."

Two years ago *Happy Days* was caught in the vacuum of failure, out of the sacred top forty of the Neilsen-rated TV shows. Something had to be done, and it was decided to enlarge the character of Fonzie in his relationship with Richie, played by Ronnie Howard. It worked, and The Fonz moved in above the Cunningham garage. As Fonzie grew so did the show's ratings, and ABC suggested to Paramount Studios, the owner of the show, that more scripts should be focused on Fonzie.

Still, Hoffman says: "Henry doesn't want all the lines or the plot in every show. He wants the relationship (between Fonzie and Richie) to pay off. You see," Hoffman told *Crawdaddy* Magazine, "The key is, The Fonz is untouchable. You just can't touch The Fonz. Only Richie can, and he'll never make the overture. If Potsie ever touched The Fonz, we'd be dead."

Hoffman added: "In the series, The Fonz helps the boys. They need him. But remember, he needs them too. They acknowledge his cool and are really his closest friends."

The work-week for *Happy Days* is Wednesdays through Tuesdays. On Tuesday night the week's particular episode is filmed before a live audience, and it is the same night that the next week's script is distributed to the cast. Each Wednesday morning Henry joins Ron Howard, Anson Williams, Tom Bosley, Donny Most, and Marion Ross on Stage 19 where they rehearse the new script under the watchful eyes of Tom Miller, Ed Milkis, and Garry Marshall, the executive producers of the show. The cast is good natured and friendly, even during pressure-filled weeks when there are a lot of rewrites on a script that's not working well.

Henry is punctual on the set, arising early each morning and waking himself with an over-sized mug of steaming tea and the morning edition of *The Los Angeles Times*. After a shave and a shower he's in his new Audi for the fifteen-minute drive to Paramount studios, home of the series.

The cast spends the first couple of days getting the week's segment "on its feet," stage-side jargon for taking the written words and combining them with the physical movements on the familiar sets of the Cunningham home, Arnold's Drive-In, and Fonzie's garage-top apartment. It's hard work and often boring as each scene is meticulously repeated over and again as the director strives for just the right movement, the right timing, the right reaction.

By Friday the actors have memorized the bulk of their dialogue, though frequently additions or deletions are made on Monday morning. The process of repeated "run throughs" continues in a never-ending effort to perfect the show. Mondays the technicians arrive, and the day is spent "camera blocking," doing the show from start to finish so the cameramen, soundmen, and the grips, the men who actually move the dolly-riding cameras from one position to another, can plot the work they'll do on filming day.

Tuesday, Henry Winkler and the others arrive at the studio at midday. The afternoon is devoted to last minute changes and still another rehearsal. The dinner break comes in the early evening, a time when a long line begins forming outside the studio, for the seven o'clock filming.

The build-up of tension among the cast resembles opening night on Broadway. Each actor has his or her own way of relaxing before the taping starts. Tom Bosley walks to Nickodell's for his dinner, a pleasant restaurant adjacent to the Paramount lot. Ronnie Howard is joined by his wife for a quiet meal at their favorite restaurant not far away. Anson Williams and Donny Most take Erin Moran (who plays Joanie on the show) for a sandwich, while Marion Ross nibbles on a salad in her dressing room.

For Henry Winkler it's a tuna fish sandwich, something he eats regularly, and a glass of tea. He's in his dressing room but he's not alone. His agent, Joan Scott, is with him. They're talking business. Someone wants to record an album with Henry. The Tonight Show wants him as a guest, and a game show producer is again ready to make whatever concessions are necessary to get Henry as a contestant. The offers keep pouring in.

Thirty minutes before filming the audience is guided into the bleacher-type seats. Backstage the actors are taking their turns in the make-up department. The conversation is focused on just about every topic other than the show, one way to relieve the tension. On either side of the large sound stage are security guards.

Joan Scott leaves her client in the privacy of his dressing room where he slowly changes his clothes. A tap on the door tells him it's time. Henry mouths the lines he is to recite in the opening scene, then takes a quick glance in the mirror. With both hands, he palms his long hair to the side of his head. He clears his throat and leaves his dressing room. He is ready, and in the few steps it takes him to walk from his dressing room to the brightly-lighted stage he becomes the person millions have come to idolize: The Fonz!

CHAPTER 9

"This Guy Is Going to Be a Star"

What makes Arthur Fonzarelli great? Henry says: "I haven't done it all by myself. I could not do it without Ron Howard—there's no way I could have done it without him. I could not do it without Tom Miller or Garry Marshall (the executive producers). People write words for me and I put them inside me, turn them around within me, and it comes out Fonzarelli."

Henry's tribute to Ron Howard is particularly noteworthy because the original premise of *Happy Days* called for Ron to be the focal point of attention with a diverse supporting cast. Today Henry Winkler has co-star billing on the show, just beneath Ron and Ron's TV father, veteran actor Tom Bosley. Regardless of the billing, however, it is obviously Henry who's captured stardom status.

Ron Howard is probably Henry's closest friend on the series. Ron has literally grown up as an actor, having gained recognition as a child on *The Andy Griffith Show*. Currently, he's collaborating with his father on a film script, and he took time off from that project to meet with me at the Smoke House restaurant, not far from his Burbank home.

"Because we're basically about the 1950s, I felt we would remain on the air for two-and-a-half to three years," he says. "I thought we'd go on at mid-season and be moderately successful coming in on the tail of *American Graffiti*. I felt we would kind of hold our own our second year and then our third year that would be it.

Nostalgia would be over and so would the show, unless we could build the show around characters, so at the end of the two-year period people would be watching not because of the gimmickry of the 50s, but because they were interested in the people.

"That's what we have done because we have a very strong cast and a good group of writers. They've balanced out the show a little bit more, taking away from the Richie Cunningham character (Ron's role) and the strength of my character, but I really think that it worked well. Everybody's had their own episode this past season, similar to the way they do it on *The Mary Tyler Moore Show,* for example. And increasing Henry's part, that was a big boost.

"Tom Miller is really responsible for bringing Henry into the show," Ron explains referring to one of the executive producers. "They wanted to bring in a big tall guy, but Tom pushed very hard to get Henry in there. Tom came up to me and said, 'What do you think of Henry?' right after the first reading. And I said, 'Well, he's really great.' I mean, even just sitting around the table reading the first script he was fantastic. He only had a few lines in the first show, and yet Tom said, 'I don't know what it is about this guy, but he's going to be a star. Whether he's going to be Al Pacino or just big in television or what, I don't know, but he's got it. I just feel it.' I didn't particularly feel that, but it's interesting that Tom would say that after one day.

"But then," Ron continues, "working with Henry on the set, you see he's largely in control of his own destiny because he's so bright. It's not a cut-throat type of thing, it's total preparation, total dedication, and a creative mind. Without rocking the boat, without making a big deal out of it, he just comes up with ideas. And he thinks, and that's how his character grew and developed. See, he didn't want to do the cliche things. You never see Fonzie comb his hair. You've never seen him roll a pack of cigarettes up the sleeve of his T-shirt. You've never seen him wear a belt with a big buckle on it. Those are just little details, but he based his character on details, and it just shows that's there's a lot to it."

Ron feels Henry is doing a professional job of accepting his new-found fame. "He's coping very well. We've had long talks about that. One day we were walking down the street near the studio, and some people came up and said, 'Heeeyyy, Fonzie.' And they talked to both of us and then we walked on and he looked at me and said, 'I can't wait til I've been in the business eighteen years so I can handle it as well as you do.'

"But really, he's done very well, and he's been bombarded. Again, because he's so intelligent, he's been able to step outside the situation and look at it from an intelligent standpoint and see it for what it is. He's been able to use it where he can use it and cope with it where he has to cope with it, discard it where he needs to discard it. As a result, he's not driving himself completely crazy."

As for the interaction between Ron's character and Fonzie, the actor says: "Richie is the only character that Fonzie will let his hair down with, take a problem to, open himself up to. Now Richie will kind of go along out in public with being set back by him and everything, but they have a close relationship.

"There was one time when I was doing *The Shootist,* a John Wayne movie. They let me out of the show to do it, but we still had two more episodes left to film so they wrote one episode where I went away to Northwestern for a journalism seminar and then another one where I came back. And the one in which I came back turned out to be what I thought was one of my stronger shows because Rich really had a purpose. He came back and Fonzie was supposed to start wearing glasses, and he was saying, 'I can't wear glasses; if Richie was here I could wear them.' And I came walking in and I said, 'Look, you need glasses so you should wear them.' So he put the glasses on and that was that, and I enjoyed that because I like having that type of relationship between Richie and Fonzie."

Henry has told *Crawdaddy* Magazine: "I'll give you a tribute to Ron Howard. There is this show called *Almost Anything Goes*; it is for buffoons. A guy slides down a board, there is a guy next to it in a Western outfit at a bar. He slides a glass of beer into some mud or something. Anyhow, Ronnie and I were asked to go on it. Now I'll go if he will. But Ron says, 'Richie can roll around in the mud and make a fool out of himself; the Fonz can't.'"

Henry told me: "Ronnie is a very good friend of mine, a good friend. He knows I'm not in competition with him. He has respect for me and I have respect for him.

"Ronnie is determined to become a film director and really isn't that interested in becoming any bigger a star than he already is, which is sizable in its own right. When the producer came up to him at the start of the season and told Ronnie that I had been moved up to co-star, Ronnie gave me a big hug and a handshake.

"Now in the show, the fact of the matter is, if Richie wasn't so square, Fonzie couldn't be so cool. Ron and I work together like we've done it all our lives. In twenty minutes we can take four pages of a script, memorize it, rehearse it, and shoot it just like that." He snaps his fingers.

"See, Ron is just twenty-one years old, but he's much older than his years reflect. He is thoughtful, and he is thought-filled. He's a sincere man, and he's going to be a great director in this business some day. He's already making films with his own money, but that's just the beginning. You wait, he's just getting started."

There appears to be an equally solid relationship between Henry and the show's other actors. Anson Williams says, "He's going to get great movies because he's a great actor." Williams has gained recognition in his own right as a result of frequent appearances on TV variety and talk shows. "I think as an actor the show has probably helped Henry more than anyone else. I don't think it gave me the tools to go out and be terrific as it has Henry, but I think it opened the garage door so I can get to the tools."

As for working with Henry and knowing the attention he receives, Anson, who portrays Potsie, says: "I don't see how anybody can be jealous because somebody's good at something. I thought it was terrific when Henry got that movie, *Katherine,* and he thinks it's super that I'm cutting my first record. The show's a very happy family."

Donny Most, Ralph on *Happy Days,* adds: "From the beginning it seemed to be more than just a normal thing. We got along very well, everybody in the cast has, and we still have a great relationship."

Most does concede that Henry's popularity

has had an effect on himself and probably the rest of the cast. "The effect, I think, is trying to keep it in perspective. I mean, when you see someone else getting all that, if you didn't respect that person then there might be a basis for resentment and that kind of thing. But I feel so strongly about Henry as a friend, I'm so happy for him and I'm happy that he's handling it. It's incredibly hard to be under the gun that he's been under. Even for me, it's been difficult trying to adapt to certain things, keeping my perspective. His pressures are ten-fold the impact of mine, but he's handled it great."

Another indication of their friendship is the red director's chair that sits in Most's Sherman Oaks apartment, where he and I talked. The chair's backrest reads Ralph in white letters with a miniature hot rod beneath the name. Across its back is printed Donny Most. The chair was Donny's birthday gift from Henry Winkler.

CHAPTER 10

"Fonzie Is, at Heart, a Hero-Worshiper"

The Fonz can be a springboard for Henry's future or, as he has said, it can be its death. On the list of his life's priorities his career is still listed number one, and most of his energies are directed at sustaining it. With this in mind, it's easy to understand why he insists that his billings always be in his own name.

When a magazine publisher approached him with the idea of a publication about him, Henry co-operated only when it was agreed that the title of the magazine would be, *Henry Winkler as Fonzie*. During the '76 summer hiatus from the show, he toured Ohio with the prestigious Kenly Theatre Players in *Room Service*, his first stage play in three years—and in a role far removed from Fonzie. He's also reading scripts for different characterizations. As beneficial as The Fonz has been to Henry, he knows there has got to be something beyond it.

One step in that direction was the ABC World Premiere Movie, *Katherine*, in which Henry played the role of Bob, terrorist and Katherine's boyfriend. The film aired in October, 1975, and while it didn't gain a lot of critical acclaim, it was a diversion from Henry's role in *Happy Days*. It also showed Henry's abilities as an actor as he created another type of believable character in an otherwise dated story about youthful radicals.

The movie was billed as "a portrait of a young revolutionary," but as reviewer Thom Montgomery said, "The film's anti-heroine is straight from the pages of yesterday's news."

Still, the critic did have some good comments to make about Henry, especially when viewed from his role on *Happy Days*. "Where Sissy Spacek (Katherine) is specious, Henry Winkler is bright. The role is that of a rebel. Fonzie is, at heart, a hero-worshiper, and models himself psychologically on those great rebel heroes, James Dean and Marlon Brando, who in the fifties were, really, one of the same. Bob (Henry's role) is also a hero-worshiper, modeling himself after Che Guevera. And just as Fonzie's behavior is at once outrageous and innocent and (today) understandable, by virtue of his search for a never-found self, so Bob is a character never found.

"After all," Montgomery wrote, "Fonzie will never grow up to be James Dean or Marlon Brando. He'll most likely continue being a grease jock or sell insurance. We know that. And Bob is never going to grow up and fight battles for The Cause in the jungles of South America. He's going to grow up and sell insurance or enter some other white collar haven.

"To view Bob is to view the modern Fonzie. The subtle differences are there, and Winkler does an astounding job in bringing them forth. While throwing a bomb would be as alien to Fonzie as pushing a pencil would seem to Bob, both are doomed by their own ignorance of the future—of the future as prelude to the past.

Winkler brings out the differences—and manages nonetheless to bring out the striking similarities. As Winkler plays the role, the two young adolescents remain forever teens. As an actor, it is as though Winkler (as Bob) were searching for Fonzie. And as we know, he found him.

"It is a remarkable accomplishment."

Such accolades have become part of Henry's reputation as an actor. And delighted as he understandably is, he is also likely to say, "I've done my homework."

Henry says: "When I was in New York I would fall asleep and dream sometimes that I was on the Dick Cavett show and doing both parts. I would ask myself a question and then I would answer it. In bed, asleep, I was so lucid. Cavett's never had an interview like that in his life." He laughs. "But you never really expect it to happen.

"I'm not original in this, but since the age of fourteen I have rewritten my acceptance speech for the Academy Award every year. I'm always thanking different people. Sure you dream about things like that. Getting an award, whether it means anything or not, verifies your life.

"The biggest reward is that I'm working. There are twenty-five thousand actors or more that are card-carrying members of SAG or AFTRA or Equity (the actors' unions) and I am one of the working ones. I am successful at what I am doing, and you say a prayer of thanks for that every day.

"However, as much as I love TV, I've done it enough. Don't forget, I've trained nine years to be an actor, and my goal wasn't to do Fonzie for the rest of my life.

"Sure I could make a pile of money with the character, doing a spin-off in another series. But what would I do then? I'd be so well-known as Fonzie I wouldn't be able to be cast in another role. Money's not my motive. They tell me I could be a millionaire within three years, but that still does not enchant me. Money is really incidental. All I'm interested in is becoming a better actor.

"It's been three years since Yale and everything that I've been yelled at for, all the criticism I've gotten, is starting to become organic, starting to sink in. Acting is like being a brain surgeon. When you're fifty-five you get it together. I have a long way to go. The image of what I want and the ability are still apart."

To his myriad young fans, however, Henry Winkler is already very much where it's at. Even when he's brushed his long brown hair down over his ears, grown a beard, worn sunglasses, dressed sloppily—they stop him on the street for his autograph.

When he went to Milwaukee, seventy thousand fans showed up to welcome him to their city. When he made an appearance at a telethon in Hawaii, the entire island's populace came out to say "Aloha." He arrived in Little Rock, Arkansas, at 11:30 P.M. and was told five people would meet him. Two thousand screaming women, young and old, showed up. Henry says: "I was a Beatle for a moment."

Once, a woman glued herself to his side as he got off an airplane and struggled for his waiting car. Finally, politely, Henry asked if she would please let go. "No," she said. "I'll never get this opportunity again."

When a young girl in Dallas squealed, "Oh, you're so short," her comment prompted a fan magazine to run a contest entitled, "Is Fonzie Too Short for You?" Six thousand fans assured the editors his five feet six-and-a-half-inch frame was ample.

At one point, hysteria reached new highs (and lows) with reports of Henry's untimely death. His sister received a phone call telling her that her brother had been killed. A month later, Henry himself received articles from Australia reporting that he had died in an auto crash. A radio station in Omaha reported his death from an overdose of drugs. Both the Associated Press and United Press International contracted ABC Television to check on Henry Winkler's well-being.

"I have no idea how that started," Henry said

as the crazy rumor about his death spread. "I'm not interested either. If people want to think I'm dead and cause such a ruckus, I'm very flattered, except that I wish it was more positive. That kind of publicity I can do without. That's really negative energy. Death *is* negative energy."

One reporter suggested that perhaps someone was trying to make Henry into another James Dean. "I would not be so presumptuous as to think that I am James Dean," Henry snapped. "So they can't make me into Dean because he was who he was and I am who I am. I mean, he was a wonderful actor that I love, but I don't know what they're trying to do in reporting my death."

Whatever the underlying reasons for Henry Winkler's emotional impact, his effect on young people is obvious by the copious coverage his every move gets in the fan magazines. Everything from his favorite color (blue most of the time, but occasionally forest green) to his favorite recipes (pot roast, potato pancakes, chocolate mousse) is faithfully reported on. More recently, Henry's impact on the populace in general was reflected by *People* Magazine's cover story about him. *People* called him "a cult," with The Fonz being "TV's super character."

Before Henry's role Fonzie was enlarged, *Happy Days* was attracting 27 percent of the Tuesday night television audience. Today it's almost fifty. He gets three thousand letters a week, or roughly, 85 percent of the entire show's fan mail.

"It's changed my life. It absolutely freaks me out!" Henry says.

Marion Ross, Mrs. Cunningham on the series, says: "I'm watching a young actor who's going to be famous for a long time."

But Henry—being Henry—worries: "The whole thing could ruin you. It has given me a national audience, and it's given me fan mail, which I've never had in my life. I read as much of it as I can. I get boxes at a time! I went over to Las Vegas for a weekend because I'd never been there before and I walked into this casino and everybody, from croupiers to the girls serving the drinks to well," he says hesitantly for fear of boasting, "everybody, it seemed, stopped me for an autograph. An afghan in my apartment was made for me by a fan."

Nevertheless, regardless of the adulation over the Fonz, the most important thing to Henry is that people never forget he's an actor who has created a character.

"It's been a national campaign on my part to emphasize that Fonzie is my fantasy. Henry Winkler is the real person. See," he says seriously, "what you've got to do, what I've got to do, is remember that I'm Harry and Ilse Winkler's son. When you have happen to you what's happened to me you are given so much power, so much power you feel like you are God. It's an immense power, and I'm very proud of it. I do not take it lightly. I approach it, the doing of it and the responsibility of it, as I do everything in my life, with a total commitment. I do not do anything mediocre.

"But you can start to believe you are more than you are, and if you don't keep that in proportion, you're dead. If I don't keep a perspective, if I start to believe that I am more than who I am, I'm dead. I'm dead as a father, I'm dead as a husband, I'm dead as an actor. I will be dead as Henry. I will never be able to create again because I will get in the way. Now I'm not a father and I'm not a husband yet, but when I am I'd better have everything in proportion. If I'm going to bring life into this world, with the help of a woman, and if I'm going to have any kind of rapport with that woman or with that child, I'd better be exactly who I am.

"Additionally," he says, "I cannot start living an image. If I live an image I will live one day behind myself. I will never be Henry Winkler. The reality is that I've been Henry for thirty-one years, and I respond best to that. I am not Fonzie. I do not want to be him. He is my job. I love to create him, but that is where the line is drawn.

"I love my audience," Henry told a magazine interviewer, "but I can't let them rule me. I just can't live my image. But I am very proud. I am beginning to be proud of myself. I'm just starting to understand that I can respect what I've accomplished because if you put it in business terms, I have moved up the corporate scale. If I never do it again in my life, I have accomplished this.

"It's very easy to get caught up in your own importance," he reiterates. "It can start to get to you when people show you so much adulation. Your head starts getting inflated. You have to bring yourself down to earth. If I ever got so cocky, if I ever get as cool as people think I am, then everything will suffer. I'll get to feeling that I don't have to work as hard. If I get slick, I'll get boring. If I get boring, I'll lose work. It's very pragmatic.

"Let's face it," he's said frequently, "there are too many performers in Hollywood who are actors for the wrong reasons. All they care about is being invited to parties or becoming members of the jet set. There are plenty of high-priced celebrities around today who don't belong there. And their stardom replaces the homework they never did. It shows up in their work.

"All I'm interested in is becoming a better actor. As soon as *Happy Days* ends I'm going to concentrate on films.

"Sure, adulation is part of why I act, but when I'm doing the work I don't think about the adulation. I think about creating the perfect character in the sky. About creating the perfect energy. What an artist can do with his paintbrush and his imagination and his eyes, I can do. My whole body is the paintbrush."

Henry pauses a moment to catch his breath, to collect his thoughts, before returning to the topic of coping with people who stop him at airports, convention centers, or even men's rooms.

"If I have the energy to do it, why not? But also, people come and say to me, 'I like what you do with your life.' Parents say, 'You bring a lot of joy into our home. Thank you.' And I for one cannot deny that. Because if someone is going to watch me, I'll be on the air. If people don't watch me, I'll be sitting at home watching TV myself. It's all relative, so I appreciate that —and besides, it's fun to be with people.

"However," he says, "there are those who like to be with people in the limelight. The fact of the matter is that at this moment, I'm in the limelight. So there are times when I have to be careful about the reasons people approach me because their intentions are not always pure. Deep down they secretly want me to be this man who I am not. The Fonz is a character; he's bigger than life, and I am not. Sometimes hostile people will come up and say: 'Well, if you don't want to be recognized, stay in your house. Here, please sign this.' They want to get you before you get them."

CHAPTER 11

"I Think the Fonz Will Get Married Some Day"

For all their obvious differences, a great deal of Henry Winkler emerges when he discusses The Fonz. Although Fonzie maintains multi-relationships with the girls (as does Henry), the actor sees his fictional character with marital ambition (as he sees himself).

"I think The Fonz will get married some day," Henry says. "But at the moment he's too young. It doesn't matter that people married younger in the 1950s. The Fonz understands that marriage is a responsible position to be in, and you'd better know what you're doing."

When I spoke to him about his own relationships with women, Henry said: "I have plans for marriage. I just don't have definite plans at the moment. I look forward to the day when I can have my woman in our collective bed. And then of course she can get up and do whatever she wants. I've even defined what I need from a woman. I need someone who is intellectual enough to have her own life and open enough to be in love with me. And I've defined love as being supportive enough to allow me to meet my potential. But I want to live with somebody, not live through somebody.

"It takes a lot of work to have a relationship with another human being that you live with in the same house over an extended period of time; that you share your life with; that you are vulnerable with; that you are not perfect with; that you love; that you are angry with; that you laugh with. At this moment in my life, my career is just beginning to unfold, and it would be a difficult thing for me to settle down. I won't be able to do that until I can make that commitment, take that responsibility for myself and the woman who is my wife.

"There are times when I'm more mental than I am emotional," he adds, "even though I am a highly emotional person. Certainly I would like a lady with a sense of humor. I would like a woman with her own point of view, her own opinions. I would like a woman who could understand that you can be angry but still be very loving, still be very much in love.

"It is my hope that when I do marry it'll be just a one-time experience. I won't say that I'll be married only one time because I don't know that. There are a lot of variables. You can't really control what's going to happen in your lifetime, but I would like to live with and grow up with just one woman one time and have an environment in which there is a nice, comfortable flow between everybody in the family—between the wife, the children, the animals, whatever there is."

In a recent magazine interview Henry was asked whether he and the character he plays have similar ideas about girls and marriages. Henry said:

"There was this episode where Fonzie almost got married. Fonzie had a list of requirements for his prospective bride—Number Four was 'untried.' Now there are very few modern-day men of thirty or thirty-one who seriously would have that requirement—that the wife be a virgin when they are married. Certainly we all know that the person we meet has a history before we get there. And that person's history is important because it helps us understand why that person is the way he is or she is today. And that's the only reason."

The article mentioned that Henry wouldn't mind taking out the garbage and washing the dishes when he married.

"That's true," Henry says. "I sincerely believe that. I can remember being in my apartment in New York and opening the refrigerator to get a sandwich and there was a bottle of apple juice staring at me. That's all, just a bottle of juice. How come? All my life there'd been food in the refrigerator, the sheets had been changed, my laundry was done. How was that accomplished? Who did it? A magic fairy? No. The thing is that it gets done because *you* do it. For yourself. Not because you expect somebody to do it for you. I don't believe you marry a girl and make her into a maid.

"The important thing is that I would be very happy to be a part of my own household, a part of the flow of making things work. And I cannot see where the woman is destined to serve only me. Certainly with my emotional needs, I need a dedicated woman, but I also need a woman with a life of her own. You can tell if a girl is committed to you. She can do whatever she wants in the world and you are very secure and you can feel that.

"I like doing dishes. It allows me time to think and it also accomplishes something. Taking out the garbage is a chore I've had since I was a little boy at home. Why not continue doing that? It's fun to see everything sparkle and shine.

"Girls write to me and say, 'Listen, I wouldn't mind waiting fourteen hours a day at home for you.' They know I work a long day at the studio. I get up at six in the morning and work isn't finished until six or seven that night. No, a girl wouldn't mind—for about two days. Then she'd be saying, 'Well, I'm sitting here all by myself. Can I have a friend over?' Nobody looks at the reality of the situation. They only see the romanticism, which has got to be balanced."

Being fair with women is something Henry has learned as an adult. When he was younger, he used to deposit his dates in a corner while he visited with friends at parties. Today, he's very attentive to the girls he dates, very "upfront" honest with them.

"I put my cards on the table immediately," he says. "I tell them exactly where I'm at at the moment, what I'm feeling. Everybody knows everything that goes on. Either I am not dating you exclusively or I want to date you exclusively and we'll go on from here.

"It's true that dating someone in the business is easier because she's more aware of the tensions and the problems," Henry says, "but you can also find somebody who can deal with the amount of tension that is generated from being a 'celebrity' who is not an actress.

"There are some women who are freaked out by it. I mean, if I am out with a girl who is not in the business and I am stopped by a lot of people she does not know how to relate to that. It can be scary, all those people coming at you. Being associated with a TV personality can also be titillating to some women. I have to be careful. Sometimes I'll see a girl in a restaurant and she'll say, 'Oh Fonzie, I dropped my fork!' She'll actually yell it out. So you become very weary of who is with you because you're Henry Winkler and having a good time, and who is with you because you're a TV star. I have to remain objective with a woman a lot longer now, because this town is filled with women who only function in direct correlation to the amount of power a man has. That's a bummer to me."

Henry's also had some "bummers" with women because of his religion. Arthur Fonzarelli is Italian, but Henry Winkler happens to be Jewish. And that can make a difference.

"I'm very proud of my religion," Henry says. "I'm proud of the heritage, the history of my religion. But I'm aware that other people have their own religion, and believe they should have it, whatever it is."

Henry's dated a lot of non-Jewish girls, and not all of the experiences have been good.

"When I was at Emerson I dated a girl who lived in the South. I liked her very much. We had good relationship until I made a trip to her home town to meet her parents. I was from New York. I was an actor. And I was a Jew. They were all prepared not to accept me. I didn't see her after that visit."

Such experiences have made Henry think that he probably couldn't marry outside his religion. He says: "No matter what happens, there is always an underlying prejudice against it from one religion or the other, whether you can feel that on the surface or not.

"Still, I date a lot of non-Jewish girls, so I don't know for a fact that it's really true. And I wonder if some of my thinking comes from feeling that it would not please my parents. I think my parents would accept anybody that I brought into the family, but I'm sure they'd much prefer it if the girl were Jewish."

Nevertheless, Jewish or not, Henry admits that his biggest problem with women is his own emotional set-up.

"I get shy when I'm emotionally involved. I can't eat. I don't sleep. I get diarrhea," he says. "When I'm not that interested, or when I don't know that I'm that interested, I live my life with abandon."

Otherwise, he says, he has given too much of himself to women in the past, "too much power," as he would put it.

There was a time when he was living in New York and shared an apartment with a designer-girlfriend. Henry says their relationship was so one-sided he used to have to reintroduce himself each time he arrived home.

"I'd go, 'Hi, it's me again. I'm still the same weight. I'm wearing the same clothing. Remember me?' Wow. I really picked winners, and that's when I realized no person is worth that much power. You allow them to do it, so you've got to get it together. See, when you have a relationship with someone you want it to continue. You want it to last so you put a lot of feeling into it. But then what's happened to me is I'd hear, 'I don't want to do that,' and I'd think, 'All right, let's not do that. Let's do something else.' I kept giving up all the time."

In his most honest moments he admits that he has some of the same habits today. Although the move from New York to Hollywood allowed him time for "self-discovery" with women, he confesses that even today he can see himself falling into the pitfall of giving up too much.

"I can be involved with someone for just a few months and see it coming," he says with an amused grin. "I'll say, 'Okay now, you don't have to go through this.' Now, whether I can extricate myself or not is not even the issue. That I get myself into it is laughable. It's laughable that I keep getting myself into these situations.

"The thing of it is, I've learned that I care in the wrong place more than that I care too much. I'm sure that there are women who would be just as happy with who I am and what I do, but I've simply never found them. When I am out of all these syndromes I'll probably be able to settle down."

CHAPTER 12

"We're Just Good Friends"

The young woman Henry Winkler had most recently dated "almost exclusively" is Jaime Lynn Bauer, who plays Lauralee Brooks on daytime TV's *The Young and the Restless*. Henry and Jaime went together for about six months.

"Jaime and I are just good friends," Henry tells me. Then he grins. "I can't believe I'm saying that sentence. I cannot believe I just told you that 'we are just good friends' because that is what I've read in fan magazines all my life. Now I know why I've read it—it's the truth!

"It's funny. It's really funny that I am now part of this life that I have heard about. You know, that's another thing that freaks me out. That I am in the middle of this life that one only hears about and doesn't really think they're ever going to be in."

In her own individualistic way, Jaime Lynn Bauer is part of that life too. I talked to her about Henry in her Hollywood hillside home, with its panoramic view of Los Angeles and—on rare smogless days—of the Pacific Ocean. Jaime is a forthright and candid young woman, who says she needs independence and "space" in which to live.

"I met Henry at the Los Amigos Children's Hospital benefit, at Christmas, 1974," she says. "I was terrified, because I'd never been to one of those things before. I was standing there, didn't know anybody, and wouldn't recognize a star if I saw one. Then I see this very Yale-looking guy, this Eastern-type of guy, with his little tie, shirt and jacket, and dark slacks, standing near-by—standing like Henry does, totally unlike Fonzie, his head sort of down and his hands crossed in front of him.

"I just stood there because I'm kind of shy with strangers, and because Henry and I both seemed kind of lost. So he sort of started talking to me and I kind of started talking to him and we talked for a long time, the whole bus ride to the hospital and back. We talked about every-thing, including my relationship with Mark [at-torney Mark Evans whom Jaime was dating at the time and continues to date today]. I think Henry called a couple of times but I wasn't interested.

"Then," she continues casually, "I did a guest appearance on the TV show, *Kate McShane,* at Paramount Studios, and I ran into him. At that meeting he was really into Fonzie. It was funny. He saw me, and it was really funny be-cause he was being very cool, not being Henry but playing Fonzarelli. He grabs me like Fonzie would and gives me a kiss. He was playing this role, a he-man trip, and I'm shocked.

"He said something that made me feel kind of bad because soon after we'd first met I'd gone with a girl friend of mine to his house and spent a few hours talking with him and listening to music. But that had been it. I didn't see him again for another eight months when I ran into him at Paramount, and he's really coming on and I'm really taken back. But I was sort of intrigued, actually " she laughs, "and yet I kind of felt embarrassed because I didn't want to hurt his feelings.

"I hadn't rejected him. I just wasn't into that space at the time. So I said, 'Listen, here's my number, call me.' Things weren't going very well with Mark, and I was living with a girl friend and her sister and everything was very complex, not very happy. Then one day I was just feeling in the mood for a walk in the park and so I did something I never do, which is stop by someone's home unannounced. Fortunately, he wasn't home so I just left a little note on his door. I wanted him to go for a walk with me.

"He called me from the note and we started talking and made plans to go out. I was totally shocked by the fact that I really liked him. I really had a good time and I found that I was very attracted to him, which I had never sensed before."

Jaime points out that Henry was being Henry now, not Fonzie. Then she goes on: "So we started seeing one another—a lot! I was rather shocked at myself actually because usually if I meet a new man I hold him off and I see him maybe once a week, or twice maximum. But I keep really cool and let the relationship grow very slowly."

That was not true with Henry. He and Jaime were practically inseparable from the very beginning.

"I guess it was because Henry was in the business," Jaime explains. "I'd never been into actors before, and he apparently had never been into actresses before. He likes to talk. He likes to try and understand. He likes to try and communicate and we got very much into that; into feelings and into talking. As a matter of fact, I revealed more to Henry than I ever have revealed to anyone. He was very sweet, warm and affectionate.

"And I could escape from that madhouse of three women, run to Henry's, and study my script without being hassled. I mean, we could share the same room and he could do paperwork or watch television or listen to music under his earphones, and I would study my script. He was very encouraging to me; he gave me great encouragement. He gave me comfort and affection, and he was there for me. Very supportive, as I was for him.

"He wanted desperately to do films, as he still does, and a film offer would come up or something and I'd say, 'No, you shouldn't do it. You've got too much talent to do it. I know you're eager to do films but you're going to ruin yourself. Stop, right now. You must wait for the right film, a big film, or otherwise you are going to mess yourself up. You're never going to make the transition from television to films. You must be very careful. Don't sell yourself short, you are too good.'

"He listened, every time," Jaime says matter-of-factly, "and then came a project some people wanted him to do and we discussed that. He would say, 'I'm only going to do two shows, that's it.' And he would discuss money with me and I would say, 'No, that's too low. Ask for this much, you can get it.' And he'd say, 'Oh no, I could never ask for that,' and I told him, 'Yes, ask for it; you'll get it. Don't cut it low.' He got it."

By this time they were seeing each other "day and night," Jaime says, although few people outside of their immediate friends knew they were even dating.

"He would send me flowers and he would leave me sweet little notes," Jaime says, smiling. "Our answering services and the pages at ABC and CBS were going crazy because I'd call up and say, 'Send Henry kisses from Jaime.' And Henry would call, but we could never reach each other when we were at the studios so he'd call CBS and the page would come over to me and say, clearing his throat 'Uh, Henry called, and, uh, well, uh, I'm supposed to give you a kiss.' And I'd say, 'Far out,' and he'd say, 'Well, I can't, I mean, I . . .' and I'd say, 'Please, it's all right.' And it was so delightful for me because it was such a different relationship.

"We got very heavy for a time," she adds. "I really had a love for Henry. I remember going to look at a house he was thinking about buying and the first thing he said after we left was: 'How do you feel about the house?' And I said, 'Well, I don't like the way it's done right now, so it's hard for me to really vibe on it. It's very beautiful. I think probably with a lot of changes you could be happy here, but it's not a house for children.'

"He said, 'Why not?' I said, 'Well, look at the backyard, it's not safe for a child. It's just not a place for children.' Children are very important to me. More and more, for a time, since things weren't going too well with Mark, I thought I was going to go with Henry for a long time. Henry and I even sort of talked back and forth on maybe living together. But we talked it out and it was a mutual agreement not to. He realizes how independent I am and I realize how conventional he is. He also understood how liberal I am. So we agreed that unless we really knew for sure that that's what we wanted to do we shouldn't do it. Unless we were really ready to make that type of commitment we'd better not. We agreed that there'd be some times that I'd want to take off with a friend and I wouldn't call him and he'd be freaked out because he wants somebody to report in to him. I've never reported in to anyone in my life. You've got to understand I've never had a family. I've never had anyone to take care of me which is what the attraction with Henry was. He did take care of me, but it was frightening to me too."

Jaime was also unsettled by Henry's friends.

"In the beginning we spent a lot of time alone," she says. "I'm very laid-back—I like to stay at home. I don't like to be out among a lot of people. It's difficult for me. Every time we'd go out, after a while, there were all these people around. Every time we'd go out there'd be a new couple, or four new people, and it started to cause problems."

Jaime recalls that there were days when Henry would pick her up after a full work day on *The Young and The Restless* set, days in which she had many scenes that called for her to cry. Shortly after dinner, Jaime would want to go home and rest. She'd ask Henry to call her a cab. She remembers that he refused and agreed to leave with her instead.

In the car, Jaime would say: 'You're being insecure. I can sense it. It's not that I don't want to be with you, I do want to. But I'm very tired and I can't be with all those people anymore.' Henry would reply: 'I guess you're right. I thought that you didn't want to be with me.'

And Jaime said, "Henry, I adore you. I want to be with you, but give me a break. I'm not like you. You're easy with people. You have all these friends and you see them all the time. I don't. It's hard for me. If we're going to go out and be with other people, then give me the same two people for a second time or a third time, let me get into them, get to know them, and then the rest won't be so overpowering for me.

"I would reassure him. He would misunderstand for a moment, thinking it had to do with him when it really had to do with me."

"He was very good," she says now, "because we could talk about things like that, we could be honest with one another and we could talk things out."

Still, if there's one thing that made a deep impression about Henry it was his own admitted insecurity.

"The strange thing about Henry is that he obviously didn't have a good thing with his parents," Jaime says with typical frankness. "And he didn't live the normal New York street life with the influence of gangs and so forth where one usually develops insecurities. Henry was upper middle class. I assume he was very protected. He has no awareness of reality. He's a very learned person, but he hasn't experienced the reality of what goes on in this big wide world."

In contrast, Jaime's father left his wife and four children. The family was not well-to-do. Her mother worked two jobs seven days a week, with little time or energy left for her children. By the time she was 12, Jaime's two older sisters left her with the responsibility of raising her smaller brother, as well as with the house-cleaning, washing and ironing.

"Henry and I are opposites in many ways," she says. "Henry never knew what hard knocks are, though he's had his pains and his emotions. But he didn't grow up in the world of rough knocks. Yet he has a very negative attitude. Sometimes I would say something and he'd answer: 'That was really an unkind thing to say.' And I'd say, 'Henry, that's not what I mean at all.' He would misinterpret and when I'd tell him what I meant, he'd just say, 'Oh.'"

Jaime hesitates for only an instant before admitting that she and Henry were in love.

"I think so. I was. I would say, 'I love you.' Henry was afraid of saying, 'I love you.' But I think a great many men feel differently about saying 'I love you' . . . men feel that denotes a commitment; whereas I don't believe women always do. It's an expression of affection for women."

"He was not interested in a relationship at that time because of his career. He was not interested in marriage. He was not interested in children. I wanted a relationship. Because of his feelings for me, Henry seemed to be kind of confused. I think if we hadn't had some silly insecure come-down trip, he might have changed his mind. Because I think Henry did love me.

But it was very difficult because I think Henry thought I wanted to change him, and I didn't want to do that. I wanted to open him up. I needed him to be open, because otherwise I would be stifled and there would be no relationship.

"Henry is used to family. As a matter of fact, this is a very good insight into Henry. He's got his friends around him all the time. He doesn't know what it really means to be alone. He needs other people to, what's the word," Jaime searches carefully, "to reassure him of who he is.

"Unfortunately, that's what's wrong with the whole world—because no one knows the answers, we're trained from the time we're little children to believe that 'You do this and you'll get rewarded.' That's nonsense. All of a sudden everybody's insecure because if we do something that everybody else isn't doing, we feel it's wrong.

"Well, Henry needs that kind of substance from other people; he needs constant reassurance. He hasn't yet learned that we are all alone, period. That what we feel and who we are are okay because nobody has all the answers, nobody's any better, nobody's any higher or any lower. We're just who we are.

"I remember one night," Jaime continues, "we were talking about how his friends are all like him. They reassure him of himself, of where he's at. He needed a lot of reassurance from me, which I easily gave him because he's a beautiful human being, a talented, brilliant actor, and an intelligent, sensitive man. But he is not aware.

"One night he came over and a girl friend of mine was here. He brought over dinner and we sat around and talked. And after she left, he said, 'How do you know her? Where does your relationship with her come from?' He was really putting her down. Now we'd had discussions about my friends before. I mean, he would make snap judgments about my friends. 'I don't want to meet them. I don't like them.' And I'd say, 'That's not fair. You don't know them.' And he'd say, 'I don't care, I didn't like the way they talked to me.' or, 'Your girl friend seemed like she was coming on to me.' I said, 'Henry, she was teasing.'

"Anyway, he really put this girl down. I told him that she's my friend because I learn a great deal from her. I told him, 'She may have seemed uneducated to you, her grammar was poor; maybe you didn't like her brashness. But I want to tell you that her way of thinking, her life-style, her perspective of things, teach me something. She gives me something, and of course I give her something back. That's why she wants to be around me, because I teach her something.

"There's nothing in this life but other people. You do not grow unless you understand as many realities as possible because reality is totally an individual thing. Everyone has a different reality. A different perspective."

And he said: 'Yeah, I'm beginning to understand. To really be a good actor, to really make that perfect character in the sky, I must be able to understand as many other people and their realities and their perspectives as possible. So maybe I've been wrong in surrounding myself with people who are just like me. I think maybe you're right. I should be more open and less judgmental toward other people and try and understand so I can really build that perfect character in the sky.'

"I didn't say a word because he missed the point. It goes beyond acting! It goes beyond this silly business."

Jaime is not criticizing. She's just being her usual open and frank self, describing what people have said and how she's reacted to them. Besides, her obvious warm feelings about Henry preclude negativism.

"He brought me to many realizations," she says. "First of all, I was not used to having anyone take care of me. This comes from my insecurity, from never having been loved, never feeling loved. I felt he really loved me.

"Henry taught me how well I deserved to be treated. He was so good to me. He was so reassuring. He would say, 'It takes a lot of strength to do what you're doing. I'm very proud of you.'

"He taught me how it felt to be treated well.

He would just cuddle me and reassure me, and I could tell him things I'd never told anyone before and I know that he wouldn't use it to hurt me. He would at least try to understand that it was all right for me to be weak sometimes; that it was safe for me to be weak sometimes."

The relationship came to an abrupt end in the spring of 1976. Jaime insists it was due to a silly misunderstanding, something she says "was so blown out proportion it was ridiculous but it caused Henry to be hurt, which was not intentional because I would never hurt him. I love Henry. I love him as a human being. That's what I mean when you love someone, when you are in love with someone. That's what I've learned love is now. It's not chemistry. It's not in-love crazy, it's loving someone, it's respecting someone. I love and respect Henry."

Her feelings cause Jaime to continue caring about what has happened in Henry's life and career. "I'm concerned about Henry because I think all the publicity he's had will kill him. I think it'll kill the dream of making the transition to film. You cannot overexpose yourself in this business. Even though he's been saying, 'I am Henry Winkler and I am different than Fonzie' the Fonz is everywhere! And he's got two more years on that show. People are going to be tired of Henry Winkler before he ever gets out if he is not careful. That is my concern.

"Unfortunately, I have not been able to talk

to him. His business has been so intense. But I understand that because it can take up twenty-four hours a day. On the other hand, perhaps Henry doesn't know how to handle our friendship, does not know how to make the transition from a romance to a friendship. I'm not saying that I do either, but I'm trying."

Another point of view comes from Cindy Williams, who's worked with Henry in both *Happy Days*, and her own spin-off series, *Laverne & Shirley*.

"He's got such a sweet nature," Cindy says. She and Henry used to date when both were starting out. "He has a great sense of humor about himself. I've heard him talk and put himself down, but in a funny way. He also has a temper but it only lasts for a second.

"You have to understand that I didn't know Henry Winkler from Adam when I met him. People said, 'You two should get together,' and he called me. Then I watched the show maybe once before we went out. In watching him, I thought, 'Now there's a good actor.' But that's all I saw him do, so I didn't know what a following he already had. People would stare at him, but it was close enough to my doing *American Graffiti* that people recognized me too, and I'd gone through that type of thing with *Graffiti* so it didn't really affect me. I didn't realize what a superstar he was until recently.

"That's why we have such a solid friendship.

Our relationship was based totally on our just being Henry and Cindy; it had nothing to do with anything else. I'd go through craziness, like, 'Oh me, I didn't get that job.' And he'd say, 'Now, now'—he was very good at comforting. That's one thing about him. He's one of the most supportive actors I've ever worked with. He is so supportive and so much *for* actors because he knows what you've got to do. He'll help you as much as he can; his criticism is always structural."

He's also very protective when he's recognized in public while on a date. "Once we were at a Chinatown parade in San Francisco," Cindy says. "I couldn't see because there was a big crowd in front of us. He asked if I wanted him to lift me up and I said, 'No, I'll just look around the heads.'

"So we were just standing there and watching the parade through this crowd of people, and all of a sudden these girls turned around, one at a time like a chain reaction, and they gasped when they saw him. Then they started running toward him, but he was very much in control. It was really something the way people started coming toward him, and a lot of them did. I mean there were a lot of kids, and girls screaming and calling their girl friends, but Henry was very cool.

"He's so gracious with people. He told them, 'Okay, just be calm, and don't yell my name, don't yell, I'll sign an autograph. Now what is your name?' And he signed some and they stopped carrying on just as he asked them to do. But for a moment I thought, 'This is bigger than the both of us.'

"Now he's right up there, which he deserves, because he's a wonderful person. He's got such a good sense of humor. I mean, how can you play that character and not have a sense of humor? Henry's got an incredible wit. He showed me how to be cheerful in even the most adverse situations."

CHAPTER 13

"I Do Not Want to Be Small Potatoes"

Henry Winkler has come a long way from being "a nice, sheltered Jewish kid from New York." He says: "Right now I'm trying to re-evaluate exactly what I've got. What does this all mean? What kind of life is this? Is this viable? Is it productive? Is it important? I don't know. I have a feeling deep down in my soul that I will eventually walk away from this and do something else, because I enjoy very much being good at what I do. I do not want to be small potatoes, so I enjoy the fact that so many people like what I do with my life.

"I'm given an inordinate amount of power. That power is pragmatic because it will move me forward in my career. I don't dare abuse that power. The other stuff that goes with it? Well, everyone says that that's the price you have to pay. I sometimes think that it might be too expensive for a human being."

On the wall of his apartment he's hung a couple of sayings with personal meaning to him. They tell a great deal about the man.

One says: "If You Will It, It Is Not a Dream."

The other says: "Self-Respect Is the Cornerstone of Joy."

Get it on with The Fonz

Here it is! The ONLY Fonzie T Shirt designed and
copyrighted by HENRY WINKLER "THE FONZ" himself.
Don't settle for store bought imitations.
ACT NOW! Wear the OFFICIAL FONZIE T SHIRT.
Included FREE with each shirt a photograph
and handwritten note from Henry Winkler.
Available for a limited time. Don't be left out!

as seen on Dinah Shore

TV'S TOP COP!

_____ 78487 #1—SIEGE $1.25

_____ 78488 #2—REQUIEM FOR A COP $1.25

_____ 78817 #3—THE GIRL IN THE RIVER $1.25

_____ 78865 #4—THERAPY IN DYNAMITE $1.25

_____ 78912 #5—DEATH IS NOT A PASSING GRADE $1.25

_____ 78960 #6—A VERY DEADLY GAME $1.25

_____ 78996 #7—TAKE-OVER $1.25

_____ 78998 #8—GUN BUSINESS $1.25

_____ 80045 #9—THE TRADE-OFF $1.25

Available at bookstores everywhere, or order direct from the publisher.

SPACE: 1999

_____ 80184 Part 1: BREAKAWAY $1.50

_____ 80185 Part 2: MOON ODYSSEY $1.50

_____ 80198 Part 3: THE SPACE GUARDIANS $1.50

_____ 80274 Part 4: COLLISION COURSE $1.50

_____ 80305 Part 5: LUNAR ATTACK $1.50

_____ 80392 Part 6: ASTRAL QUEST $1.50

Available at bookstores everywhere, or order direct from the publisher.

POCKET BOOKS
Department SP
1 West 39th Street
New York, N.Y. 10018

Please send me the books I have checked above. I am enclosing $_____ (please add 35¢ to cover postage and handling). Send check or money order—no cash or C.O.D.'s please.

NAME_____

ADDRESS_____

CITY_____STATE/ZIP_____

SP

POCKET BOOKS

Ripley's
Believe It or Not!
Astounding, Amazing, Incredible!